Forget Your Age…You Can Do This!

How adults can achieve success in college,

or in any new endeavor, at any age.

Christine Crowe

Cover photography and editing by Alexandra Belanich

Interior formatting by Ming Gullo

ISBN-13: 978-1511522496
ISBN-10: 1511522496

Forget Your Age…You Can Do This!

How adults can achieve success in college,

or in any new endeavor, at any age.

Christine Crowe

This book is dedicated to Dave Crowe, my husband and best friend. Without your tenacious support, I would have given up, many times, throughout my journey. Thank you for your pride and for understanding how important this endeavor was for me. To Jenn, my daughter, who bought me a journal and encouraged me to put my thoughts in writing, thank you for believing in me. To Dave and Dan, my sons, thank you for listening and understanding when I needed to share my thoughts.

Because of my family, I can always say:
Life is Good!

Contents

One	Motivation	1
Two	Aphorisms as Wisdom	3
Three	Why Believe Me?	7
Four	The Lack of Time Myth	13
Five	Turn it Off! Turn it Off! Turn it Off!	17
Six	Easier Said Than Done? Of Course!	23
Seven	How Bad Do You Want It?	27
Eight	Stepping Slowly Through the College Doors	31
Nine	Gathering Support	35
Ten	Adding to the Support System	47
Eleven	Finding Your Space	51
Twelve	How to Afford Your New Venture	55
Thirteen	Knowing What's Best for You	63
Fourteen	Making the Right Preparations	67
Fifteen	Making Technology Work for You	75
Sixteen	Believing You Can	79
Seventeen	Still Believing	83
Eighteen	Lecture Halls and Holidays and Migraines, Oh My!	87
Nineteen	"C" is a Respectable Grade	91
Twenty	Change is Good	95

Twenty-one   Letting Go of Regrets   99

Twenty-two   So Many Young Ones   101

Twenty-three   What Will You Do Now?   149

Twenty-four   Final Thoughts   153

Appendix   155

Acknowledgements   161

About the Author

Christine Crowe is a dean and professor at Suffolk County Community College on Long Island, in New York. Through her years working at the college, she has taken the opportunity to speak to many adults, whether students in her classes or those seeking to begin new challenges through higher education or other fields. She has contributed to textbooks and has written an edited handbook for adults in college entitled, *Insider's Guide for Adult Learners.* Her passion is to help others achieve success, as she did, in spite of age, family obligations, or work responsibilities.

Through this book, the reader will learn how Chris started her journey as a married parent of three children at age 39. Having never gone to college, she epitomizes her belief in the ability of others, when she says in her title: *Forget Your Age... You Can Do This!*

For feedback or additional information visit:

www.christinecrowe.com

@4christinecrowe

Forget Your Age…You Can Do This!

Forget Your Age, You Can Do This!

Forget your age, you can do this!

Christine Crowe

Chapter 1

Motivation

As an adult student, either entering college for the first time or returning after years of being out of school, this new experience can be daunting. There will be many challenges and fears to overcome even before your journey begins.

It is with this in mind, that I share the following letter that was sent to "Dear Abby," years ago. I read this around the time I was thinking of what I would do when the need for homemaking and full-time parenting lessened. It went something like this:

> Dear Abby,
>
> I am 35 years old and I always wanted to be a doctor. I know that it will take me at least 10 years to go through the necessary schooling to reach my goal. By then, I'll be 45 years old. I'm not sure it is worth

putting myself through hall those years of studying and hard work. I need your help in deciding. Please tell me what you think I should do.

Signed,

Too old to start anew

Abby's reply went something like this:

Dear Too Old,

In 10 years you are going to be 45 years old no matter what. Wouldn't you rather look back and be able to say, "I did it! I'm glad I took the plunge," instead of having to say, "I wish I had started 10 years ago. I would have been finished and could have been a doctor now." Go for it!

I cannot tell you how many times I have relayed this story to adult women and men who tell me they are too old to go back to school or start a new career. They are as young as twenty-something and as old as sixty-something. Most have never been to college. Those who had attended college in the past were not ready and either failed or did poorly and dropped out. Some are married with children and feel guilty for wanting something for themselves. Some are divorced or widowed with no choice but to find their own way and be self-sufficient, while others just want to enhance their knowledge.

All are looking for answers, for support, or just to be told it is okay to do this. I was one of those people. This is why I decided to write on this subject. It is my hope that what I have to share in these pages will inspire many more men and women than I can reach personally in my daily interactions as a college educator working to help students realize their potential. My message is not only about how to do it, it is also to help others understand that they are able to do it and why they need to get started. It is intended for people who, like me, just want to re-invent themselves.

Some of you may be thinking right now, "What is different about what you have to say that I haven't heard before?" You will see as you read on. Simply put, I was the person you are. I have heard all of the sanguine aphorisms, and they are all true. I have also heard all of the cynical excuses, and they are only true if you allow them to have meaning in your life. What am I talking about? Let's get specific.

As you grow older, you'll find the only things you regret are the
things you didn't do.

Zachary Scott

Chapter 2

Aphorisms as Wisdom

Who is your muse, your source of inspiration? We have all heard those clever aphorisms at one time or another: *You can do it; Just do it; If I can do it, so can you; Play like a champion . . .* They are not just empty words; these are the motivating factors that we all need to cling to in order to get started and stay on track. Many were coined by wise, successful people throughout history whose words were the result of their own experiences. They were meant to encourage us and help us discover what we are capable of. They should be read as gifts to unwrap and examine and appreciate. If we do not at least take note of all they have to offer, we are doing ourselves a disservice. Let's look at some of these adages.

Johann Wolfgang Goethe told us, "Whatever you can do, or dream you can, begin it; boldness has genius, power and magic in it." Aside from his many contributions to literature, music, science and philosophy, Goethe, a German writer, was best known for the masterpiece, *Faust*, about a man who sells his soul to the devil for power and knowledge. Like his creator, Faust was interested in alchemy, an ancient philosophy whose tenets include transforming a substance of little value into one of great value. Isn't that what we aspire for ourselves? Although Goethe continued to release many great works throughout his life, he began his masterpiece at the age of 26; yet, the first of two parts of *Faust* was not published until he was 59. This alone should serve as inspiration, for it demonstrates that Goethe practiced what he preached.

***

Still not convinced? Maybe you're thinking you are not as smart as Goethe and would never be able to achieve your own dreams. To this, Eleanor Roosevelt might respond: "It takes as much energy to wish as it does to plan" or "The future belongs to those who believe in the beauty of their dreams. . . we must do that which we think we cannot." A wise woman, Eleanor Roosevelt was. She was an ardent defender of women's rights; she was always fighting to get women full recognition in society. Her words need no explanation. What there is to know about this revered former first lady is far too much to do justice within these pages. However, we know that Eleanor Roosevelt has left many gifts of her wisdom behind for us to become heir to.

***

Still second guessing yourself? Are you still thinking, "What if I make mistakes?" or worse, "What if I fail?" Your skepticism is understandable, so let's consider the words of Irish playwright George Bernard Shaw, who said, "A life spent making mistakes is not only more honorable, but more useful than a life spent doing nothing." Shaw was a leading figure in 20th century theatre; he may be best known for writing *Pygmalion*, a play that was later adapted into a movie and then the musical, *My Fair Lady*. But it is his humble beginnings that are not to be overlooked. Born in Dublin, in 1856, from underprivileged parents, Shaw was a self-proclaimed "typical Irishman" raised in poverty. Shaw had no consistent formal education but he believed in himself and in the civil liberties of others. Shaw was a free thinker; he was a man ahead of his time, and his advice should be heeded.

Don't let your fear of making mistakes prevent you from moving forward or from trying new endeavors. Instead, allow yourself to try; make those mistakes, and try again. Step out of your comfort zone, and become that free thinker who takes risks and maybe makes mistakes along the way. What is the worst that could happen? You try again.

***

As an example, let's take one of the most revered sports figures of the twentieth century, Michael Jordan. He will always be remembered for his amazing abilities as a successful basketball player. Often, his great mobility made him appear superhuman, earning him the title, "Air Jordan." Everyone wanted to "be like Mike," but as Michael Jordan tells us in his own words, "I've missed more than 9,000 shots in my career. I've lost almost 300 games. Twenty-six times, I've been trusted to take the game winning shot and missed. I've failed over and over and over again in my life. And that is why I succeed." Jordan succeeded by not letting his failures stop him. Instead, he fought through them and kept going. Had he given up at any point along the way, he would never have become the great player he was.

Can you see the pattern? Successful people recognize that if they are to live up to their full potential, they must accept the challenges that come up as well as the failures that sometimes plague them. The common denominator is how those failures are used to make one stronger, more determined and ultimately, successful.

As Pope John XXIII advised, "Concern yourself not with what you tried and failed in, but with what it is still possible for you to do."

Do not plan for ventures without finishing what's at hand. Leave no stone unturned.

Euripides

Chapter 3

Why Believe Me?

Why should you believe me? What makes me credible? These are questions I hope you are asking. These are questions I encourage my writing students to ask as they read any author's work of nonfiction. "Look at the writer's credentials," I tell them. "What makes this writer's words convincing? What makes him/her an authority on the subject? What do you know about the writer's background?" If the answer is "nothing" then "go and find out," I tell them.

Would you buy a computer or a television from a street vendor? I hope not. I would like to believe that the serious consumer would seek out a reputable dealership to purchase such important, high priced-products. In fact, many of us would spend hours, even days, doing research on quality and pricing before making such an important purchase. Surely, you could just pick up a newspaper and scan the ads for the best buy but isn't that also taking the seller's word without checking for credibility? You would want to make sure that the advertiser was reputable. You might check with the Better Business Bureau for consumer satisfaction. The same holds true for information being told to you. Whether the presenters are doctors, instructors or writers, make sure they are reliable before you accept their word, or follow their advice, or pass on their information as fact.

So what does this all have to do with what I have to say? Everything! Remember, I was the person you are. I am the person you can be. Of course, I recognize that we each have unique circumstances, and some of what you experience in your life may be much more difficult and challenging than what you will read here. However, my hope is that I can help you believe that you can achieve success as I did. No matter how you define me, it is important to realize that we are enough alike to be capable of reaching our goals.

***

My childhood was very ordinary. It started in a tenement apartment in Long Island City until I was five when my family moved to an apartment in an eight family building in the Park Slope area of Brooklyn. This residence required a daily climb of four flights of stairs to the top floor of a rent-controlled building.

The rooms were railroad-style with the living room at one end of the apartment and the kitchen four rooms away, following a long hallway of bedrooms in between. Being one of five children required the three girls to share one bedroom. Later, as a teenager, I was thrilled to be allowed to move into a tiny room beside the kitchen that was converted to a bedroom for me. Finally, the benefits of being the oldest sibling could be realized. It didn't matter that all I could fit in this little 8' x 8' space was a single bed and a two drawer end table. All that mattered was that it was my personal respite from the rest of the crowded residence. Today, my office at work is almost twice the size of that room, but, back then, I could not want for anything more. It didn't matter that the rumbling of the washing machine on the other side of the wall would serve as my alarm clock on some mornings, or that the reverberating sound of the dumbwaiter in the kitchen (as it was constantly being drawn up and down, to and from the cellar) was deafening. To me, it was the best room in the house, and, even today, I can look back and realize how fortunate I was.

Ours was, what I considered to be, an average working-class family for the fifties and sixties. My mother stayed at home to care for the children and the household while my father went to work to pay the bills. Having five children was not uncommon back then. Also not uncommon was the close proximity of relatives. Within a two-block area were my grandmothers, two

13

aunts and two uncles. We all went to the same church, and the cousins all attended the same school. On hot summer evenings, all would gather on a bench in front of the wall surrounding Prospect Park. Some of the older women would carry their own folded lawn chairs, while the younger generation might sit along the concrete wall behind the bench. We didn't have backyards; we had front stoops. We didn't own a car so the subway became our chauffeur to Coney Island on those rare ccasions when my mother could muster the strength to schlep all of us to the beach. Most of the time, however, we relied on an open fire hydrant for cooling off, also not uncommon growing up in Brooklyn.

The neighborhood was financially and ethnically diverse with residents who were homeowners, and those who were tenants, like us. As kids, we would hang out on the corners or on the stoops. In some ways, the stoop was like an extension of our apartment. It was to us what a backyard is to residents of the suburbs. There was never any need for children to be entertained in our neighborhood. We would play stickball in the street, chalk up the ground with hopscotch squares or bases, ride our bikes, or just make up games to occupy our time. Keep in mind; there were no home computers or video games back then to keep kids indoors. Unless you were grounded, you were outdoors. The only afternoon TV show that I stayed in for as a teenager was "American Bandstand," a dance show hosted by Dick Clark.

Sorry, I'm dating myself. If you are not in my age group, this means nothing to you; but, back then, I was glued to that show the way a lot of people are to shows like "American Idol" or other popular music shows.

Most families had three or four kids and, all of the youngest generation became friends as their mothers sat and chatted on benches inside the playground at the park at the end of our block. While their mothers passed the time together, the children would be swinging, sliding, or see-sawing just a few feet away. As they grew into the next generation, the friendships also grew; only now they were hanging out in the park without their mothers looking on. The kids I grew up with came from families with similar backgrounds; none of us had the luxury of organized activity. We did not have ballet lessons or karate, nor did any of us attend nursery school. Since this was all unknown to us, we didn't miss it. The streets and the park were our playground. Prospect Park opened up a world of endless enjoyment from sandboxes and sleigh riding, to ice skating with your friends as a teenager, to long strolls and falling in love as young adults, endless memories could be created.

***

When making these memories with the man I would eventually marry, thoughts of the future only included replicating what we knew in that little world in Park Slope, Brooklyn. Dave knew he wanted to become a cop like his father, and I always dreamed of being a mother like my mom. It was what I knew, what I admired, and what I aspired to. The thought of going to college and starting a career never entered my mind since college was not thought of as important for a woman back then, at least not in my family. Financially, it was not an option as we were all expected to graduate high school and obtain a job so that we could contribute to the family income. It wasn't something that I questioned; it was just accepted like everything else we grew up without and did not expect or miss.

It was not until much later in life, as we were living our dream, affording our three children all of the things that we never had growing up, that the realization of what more I could achieve came to light.

Dave's dream offered him the opportunity to build a fulfilling career. Becoming a New York City police officer allowed him to attend classes, expand his mind and his knowledge base, and as a result, he could utilize what he learned in a gratifying profession. For years, my dream of being a wife and mother was just as fulfilling. Living in a spacious home in the suburbs with my husband and three children who needed me, was all I needed to be happy. It was when the needing lessened that the voids began to develop and slowly broaden.

***

First, Jennifer reached the point where she no longer needed to hold mommy's hand to go outside and play in the backyard. Then, David was born and I would, once again, be needed.

Soon after our second child's birth we relocated to suburbia where our children could have their own bedroom and more outdoor space. With the added amenities came added upkeep and higher bills. Dave was now accepting more overtime to keep up with the expenses and commuting two-and-a-half hours roundtrip. In retrospect, it is easy to see how my void expanded.

Initially, I was busy and content with taking care of a new baby and a new house. Jenn had started school and during the day, David and I kept each other company while getting to know our new surroundings. In the afternoon, there was homework to be done and ballet lessons to attend. Soon, David needed and wanted my company less and began replacing our time with friends. Before long, he would be going to school, but not before Danny was born, filling the gap once more.

The days were filled with playtime, and walks with the neighbors and their kids, and trips to the library or the neighborhood gym where Danny could join other children in a nursery-like setting. Our routine continued unchanged until Danny was old enough to join activities of his own.

After school activities continued to grow as the children grew. Little League practice was added to ballet practice, to that was added jazz lessons and to Little League was added basketball. Each child had their activities that needed to fit in with homework, playtime, and the preparation of dinner.

As the children grew, their increased activities brought added expenses. Dave was still working long hours of overtime, and I was beginning to feel the guilt of needing to help out financially, but my choices were limited as I was neither ready, nor willing, to interfere with my time with the children. Danny deserved the same nurturing that his sister and brother received from me and that I received from my mom. Still, the desire to help out financially lingered. It was around this time that I learned of a friend's needs that were greater than my own. She was going through a divorce, and she needed to find a full-time job. Like me, she had young children and no extended family to help her out. Since Danny and her two girls were friends, we decided it would be mutually advantageous if I took care of her girls.

It was like having two more children of my own from 8:00 a.m. to 5:30 p.m. Like Danny, the girls were not yet in school, so where I went, three children tagged along. After school, there were now five children to keep in line and five children to pile in the car to take to activities. Still, it served the purpose for that time when parenting was my first calling. Before long, Danny would be in school, and I would come to realize that I needed something more. That's when I decided to try out a small business endeavor of my own at the local flea market. My booth included quality, inexpensive fashion accessories. It was something I enjoyed and it provided me a social outlet that would, once again, fill a void. This worked well for a couple of years, for it allowed me to bring Danny with me on days that he was not in school. However, once the flea market went out of business, I was left with the same voids.

By now, maybe you can begin to visualize some similarities if you have ever been a homemaker, or had children, or simply placed your desires aside out of necessity, or your inability to believe that you can juggle one more thing. Still, this should not be read as excuses for not finding what is right for us. Instead, bear in mind that perhaps we needed to finish what was at hand. Be that parenting, caring for a loved one, or just taking the time to discover what exactly "that" is. As Euripides tells us, we must "leave no stone unturned."

Christine Crowe

There are only two mistakes one can make along the road to truth: not going all the way, and not starting.

Buddha

Chapter 4

The Lack of Time Myth

You may be wondering how you could find the time to squeeze one more thing in. Just get started! Getting started can be simply thinking of what you would like to do for yourself, like "taking inventory." What are your interests? What are you passionate about? What are some things that you never experienced but have thought about doing? If you're thinking that takes time that you don't have, I get that! Remember, I've been there. I'm still there, and I still catch myself thinking that way every now and then. It's just easier to fall back on that line of thinking because it takes work to get to where we'd like to be, and frankly, we're just tired of everything in life being work. Am I right? That may be true but where will that thinking get you? Unfortunately, it will get you exactly where you are right now. Albert Einstein had a definition for this way of thinking. He described it as, "Insanity:

doing the same thing over and over and expecting different results."

However, my guess is that you began reading this because you were interested in discovering how to get started in spite of all of the barriers. So let me not disappoint you, but rather begin to squelch some of the excuses beginning with the biggest one of all — a lack of time!

The belief in what I call the "Lack of Time Myth" is the biggest motivation destroyer for adults. I know that life can be overwhelming at times. Some of you may have inconceivable demands being placed on you and can never imagine taking even one moment for yourself. We can juggle children, chores, shopping, cooking, cleaning, homework, after school activities, jobs, but we can't make time to cultivate (or even begin to discern) our own inner aspirations. Still, all my years of interviewing people who are in a rut have taught me that both women and men can overcome their belief in this "Lack of Time Myth" when they begin to think about where time can be found. Even small measures of time can be a valuable means to a productive objective.

I'm no different from every person I know, and I'm sure many people that I don't know. Finding time has always been a challenge until I started to change my thinking. Rather than continue to fall back on the convenient belief that I didn't have enough time, I needed to stop telling myself that and start believing that there *is* time to be found. In other words, time *is* available to us, but what are we choosing to do with it? That is exactly why I chose to write this book: to reach and enlighten even more busy adults.

So where or how do you begin? Once you begin to realize the benefits of changing your mindset, you will naturally begin to squelch the "Lack of Time Myth" on your own. You need to begin by finding those small measures of time that tend to be spent doing insignificant things, like talking on the phone for too long or, if you are like me, walking through department stores to look at nothing in particular.

Stop and take a look at your day. If you are a stay-at-home parent, did you watch *Ellen* this morning? Maybe you watched *Dr. Phil* or *Dr. Oz this* afternoon. Right there are a couple of hours that could have been spent on self-exploration of those inner aspirations I mentioned above. What about while your little one watched *Sesame Street,* how were you spending your time? I'm sure you were busy doing laundry or cleaning up clutter or reading through the mail or preparing dinner. Of course all of those chores are important, but why not take one half hour away from the time spent doing chores, and make time for you? Sit down with pen and paper, and begin writing some of your ideas down.

Maybe you work full time outside the home, and after a long day at work, you need to cook dinner and help the kids with homework. Perhaps one or two lunch hours a week can be spent shutting yourself off from others to discover your answers. If you have an office, close the door and take the complete hour to think about how to get started. If that's not possible, take a walk by yourself, and just think about what it is you want to do or change or explore. Find what works for you. It doesn't have to be a full hour; a half hour or even just 15 - 20 minutes can be productive. Just be sure to write things down so your ideas don't get lost in the crowded hours of your busy day. I can tell you that I have notes written in journals, on my iPhone, on pads at work, on notes on my nightstand and even on napkins. While I do my serious writing on my laptop, I always make sure to carry a small journal with me when I'm traveling because it's always when you least expect it that ideas will come to mind.

Soon you will begin to realize that you can find time for yourself that you had not thought of before. It's so easy to become overwhelmed by the many demands that are placed on you, but it is important to remember that you deserve this. Taking the time for self-exploration is important for your future and for what you would like to achieve. Don't worry about having all of the answers or knowing exactly where the road will take you, just concentrate on getting started. Even as I began my journey, still caring for our three children, I believed that childcare was all I knew; it is what I did best. I wondered what I could do with that experience. So many questions ran through my mind once I opened it up to possibilities. "Was I too old?" "Would I have the time?" "Would I be able to see it to its end?" And "What will "it" be?" I realized very quickly that I was getting ahead of myself before I had even begun.

Just as I had to do, you need to stop thinking about the end result, and concentrate on the getting there, the journey. George Elliot tells us, "It is never too late to become what you might have been."

God has promised forgiveness to your repentance, but he has not promised tomorrow to your procrastination.

St. Augustine

Chapter 5

Turn it off! Turn it off! Turn it off!

Turn off the television! Turn off the computer! Turn off the iPhone and iPad! Log out of Facebook and Twitter! Have I left out anything else that will cause you to procrastinate? If so, turn it off! Television was once the only deterrent, but today's technological advances have extended the list of preventative measures far beyond what many of us can even relate to.

According to a 2009 Nielsen Three Screen Report, Americans are now watching 151 hours of television a month, through viewing on computers, cell phones and TV. That translates to more than five hours a day! In 2014, Nielsen reported that Americans now own about four digital devices and spend 60 hours a week consuming content across these devices.

For most of us, that's our entire free time outside of work and sleep. Let's do the math. The average worker spends eight hours on the job and one to two hours travelling. They probably take up to an hour getting ready in the morning before getting out the door and an hour after returning home, up to, and including, dinner. Add to that seven hours of sleep and we're up to 19 hours in a 24-hour day. So if we're watching an average of five hours of television a day, that's our full 24-hour day. Of course there's no time for anything else in your life. Or is there?

Al Roker was asked recently how he finds time to write books. He explained that he stopped watching mindless television and replaced it with his writing. His words hit a nerve, motivating me to do the same.

My average TV watching was, at times, surpassing the national average. I'd have the TV on from the minute I woke up to check the news and weather of the day and it would remain on while I was getting ready for work. In the evening, the TV was on again to catch up with the news of the day followed by sitcoms or favorite reality shows. There were many that I'd become hooked on.

There were times when I would be sitting on the couch watching television and thinking about what I could and should be doing. I could be working out. I could be reading. I should be writing. When I finally turned off the television, I started writing again. All of a sudden, I found that there was time to do all three of the above.

***

Turning it off doesn't mean you actually have to get rid of your TV, or never again watch your favorite shows; but you should learn to set limitations on everything that stands in the way of achieving your goals to success, regardless of what that is for you. I still have a few favorites that I must DVR each week, but I've learned to limit them to a choice few. That allows me the flexibility to watch them when I have the time, or when I may need to take a break for mindless activity. I still keep the TV on in the morning as I'm getting ready, but in the evening, I'll only watch what I can fast forward through on the DVR, and only after I've spent adequate time doing what's important to me. It's all about time management.

We say we don't have the time. We think we don't have the time, and we believe it too. But the reality is that our time just needs to be managed better. We need to say and think and believe that we really do have the time. We can only do that when we learn how to manage our time much the same way we must manage our finances. For me, the television was only part of my distraction— albeit— a big part, but there was more to my procrastination.

***

As a late bloomer, living a somewhat limited life as homemaker and parent, I was not introduced to the computer until I was in my forties. Before then, we had an Underwood typewriter. Some of you may be old enough to remember that. As a student working towards my bachelor's degree, there were many papers to write, and typing them on a typewriter meant having to retype the entire paper when revisions were required. My major was social studies so there were many papers to write and revise.

Little by little, the computer was becoming popular as the preferred instrument for writing. Once one was introduced to this remarkable invention, there was no turning back. The now obsolete typewriter was quickly becoming a relic.

Initially, I made frequent visits to the labs at school to work on my papers, but that proved inconvenient, compelling my family to make the investment to purchase our first home computer. I remember sitting in front of this foreign object feeling somewhat intimidated by what I didn't know about it. It had become one of those daunting tasks that required patience and a step-by-step-by-step approach. Eventually, learning did occur, and my assignments became easier to complete. Still, it wasn't all perfection.

Back then, computers were big and clunky and work had to be saved on what were called "floppy disks" that had to be treated with care. There were no laptops to speak of, and the internet was still an unfamiliar entity only known to a select few with the technological knowhow. The moment I became introduced to the internet remains ingrained in my mind.

Those of you old enough to remember life before the existence of the internet will recall the intensive manual exploration needed to accomplish academic research. One had to physically visit the library and pour through endless card files and read through infinite articles and browse microfiche films to find information pertaining to a subject. When information was located, it may have been housed at another library. In that case, the file had to be ordered and could take up to a week before reaching its destination. It is with that in mind that I was introduced to the internet search engine, Yahoo, and for me, that was a momentous occasion.

It was in a graduate history class that one of the students volunteered to demonstrate this new discovery to our instructor and the rest of the class. The fascinating discovery that played out before our eyes was something none of us had ever witnessed. We could only stare in awe at the history being displayed before us. It was like being part of the audience in a magic show. Anything you asked, it would produce for you.

Soon after, we connected to the internet via dial-up service for our home computer through the local library before eventually purchasing a provider that would insure us uninterrupted quality access to this brilliant discovery, allowing the entire family to benefit from the knowledge acquired through this Information Super Highway.

Conversely, the hours spent idly surfing the net for other than academic purposes continued to be another means of procrastination for me, right alongside the television. Then there was Facebook.

Initially, I balked at Facebook, criticizing those who were on it as having no life. Of course, that's not a fair analysis now that I've come to realize the value of corresponding with friends and relatives through social media. It's hard to ridicule technological advancement that provides the ability to connect with people across the country, or even across the world. Instead of talking to distant family members only at weddings and wakes, we can learn what they're up to through postings on Facebook, allowing the viewer to have a virtual part in weddings, births, vacations and more, through photographs posted instantaneously.

Recently, I had the pleasure of meeting three lovely visitors on holiday from England. We all shared an immediate bond that has been able to continue through Facebook. Facebook afforded me the ability to congratulate Jackie when she graduated from nursing school, and see pictures of Sophie's newborn baby boy, and follow Melissa's journey through her visits to many exotic countries in Asia. So why is Facebook a problem?

The issue is not in the intrinsic nature of this social network, but in the manner in which we use it. I still enjoy Facebook, but now it doesn't take priority over the more important things in my life. Now I can go for days without checking it, then spend only a few minutes catching up on what my friends and family are doing, click on a few newly- posted photographs and then log off. There are those who can't let a moment of their day pass without posting a status update. Apparently, there are many who enjoy knowing what all their "friends" had for dinner. Much like the concept of Facebook, Twitter, another social network, encourages the user to send out constant "tweets" on any and all subjects of interest at any given moment. While both networks can, and have been used as a teaching medium, the user stands the risk of becoming addicted in the same way that one can become addicted to television, the internet, video games and the like. So if you are hooked on any of these technological mechanisms, what are you keeping yourself from doing? Franklin D. Roosevelt suggests to us: "It isn't sufficient just to want—you've got to ask yourself what you are going to do to get the things you want." To that I respond, turn it off!

He who would learn to fly one day must first learn to walk and run and climb and dance; one cannot fly into flying.

Friedrich Nietzsche

Chapter 6

Easier said than done? Of course!

I recall sitting in a diner one afternoon with two of my college friends, and one of them asked: "Where do you see yourself in ten years?" My first thought was, "Are you kidding? Where will I be ten years from now? I'm not sure of my life at the end of this semester." "OK, how about five years from now? Really, think about it, you must have some idea about where you'd like your life to be." All I could come up with was, "In five years, my daughter will be in college, and both my boys will be in high school and . . ." He cut me off right there. "I said where would you like to see *your* life in five or ten years?" He hit a nerve. I'd never taken the time to ponder that thought. Like many women, my life was about my family, my marriage and my children. It was as if I didn't have an identity of my own.

Even at that point in my life, having just turned 40 and attending college for the first time, I was still unable to fully envelop myself in the reality of what was my own endeavor. It never occurred to me that I had taken such a major step for my own future. Perhaps allowing myself to think that way would seem selfish. My motivation stemmed from the desire to make a decent salary, so I could contribute financially to the household. Even then, I was fully aware of the lack of importance society placed on homemaking and motherhood. I remember thinking that nothing I had done for the past 15 years could be helpful on a resume.

So how does one go from being that homemaker and mother to achieving a successful career after age 40? Let me correct that and say, at any age. Well, to begin with, you need to "forget your age" and believe "you can do this" and just get started. Or as Cher proposes, "If you really want something, you can figure out how to make it happen."

Easier said than done, you say? Of course, isn't everything in life easier said than done? Have you given birth? Or know someone who has? The very thought of it is frightening. I have given birth three times and can honestly say that attaining my master's degree was easier. When my daughter was pregnant and getting closer to her due date, she had to attend one of those dreaded hospital orientations that included a video of childbirth.

She called me in a panic and said if she weren't pregnant, after having seen this, she would never have become pregnant. Still, she got through it like millions of other mothers before her and millions who will follow. But was it easier said than done? Of course! When we plan to start a family, aren't we concentrating on what it will be like to have a little bundle of joy? I don't know anyone who wanted to become pregnant to experience the "joy of childbirth."

Life is filled with difficult challenges that are easier said than done. Have you helped a child learn to read or ride a bike? It's an experience fraught with panic and excitement. There is the aspiration to achieve success, but with that goes the anxiety, the apprehension, the alarming feeling of failure on the part of the student, or the child in this case. Still, difficult though it may be, only perseverance can bring the student to victory. It has to start with a slow, steady pace. If it's reading, it's word, by word, by painstaking word. If you're old enough to remember the classic Elson-Gray basic readers, "Fun with Dick and Jane," you'll recall reading lines like: "See Spot." "See Spot run." "Run, Spot, run." The slow, steady, sustained rate is what allowed the learner to achieve success. A new learner of any age would not be encouraged to attempt *Plato's Republic* before gaining recognition of the basic building blocks.

Similarly goes the task of learning to ride a bike. The young child who climbs up on that skinny seat for the first time has to be terrified of falling, terrified of his mom or dad letting go. Yet he knows that if they don't let go at some point, he will never be able to ride that bike alone. So the parent holds on and runs alongside the bike, over and over, until one day both parent and child feel comfortable with the parent letting go. Initially, this may result is the child falling. The routine is repeated, over and over, with the child riding freely a few feet more each time until, finally, he succeeds. Eventually, he is riding up and down hills all over the neighborhood. Of course, the parent never doubted for a minute that the learning would occur, but knew it would take a slow steady pace, and a lot of confidence on the child's part, and patience on the parent's part. Even William Shakespeare knew that learning would occur when he wrote: "To climb steep hills requires slow pace at first."

Initially, these tasks seem daunting, yet we only have to look around to know they are accomplished every day. We tell our children that it's ok to fall down and to fail. We tell them to just pick themselves up, and try again. As adults, we need to remember our own advice. We need to practice what we preach. When your own words aren't enough, find inspiration through the words of others as I have offered you. Perhaps these spoken by the great Irish playwright and author, Samuel Becket, may suffice in times like this: "Ever tried? Ever failed? No matter. Try again. Fail again. Fail better."

Christine Crowe

No one can make you feel inferior without your consent. It is better to light a candle than to curse the darkness.

Eleanor Roosevelt

Chapter 7

How Bad Do You Want It?

Whatever you're afraid of, believe that you can overcome it. I was scared to death of registering for my first college class. I showed up at the registrar with three little ones in tow. At the time, I was still a stay-at-home mom, and I was taking care of a friend's two little girls while she went off to work. So with my youngest son, Danny, and the two girls, I drove down to the community college to request a catalog and find out what I needed to do to get started. I couldn't wait to get home and start reading my way to my future. I read that book from cover to cover until I understood exactly what I needed to do.

You see, I was too insecure and afraid to walk into the admission's office and seek the advice of the counselors. I felt embarrassed to sit down with three little ones under foot. What would they think? What if they tried to talk me out of it? What if they saw the children and thought I was crazy to even consider going to school at this stage of my life? I felt inferior, and I wasn't willing to risk the humiliation. My self-confidence was already fragile, but I had come this far, and I wasn't about to turn back now. (Ironically, that same office that I was afraid to enter was the office in which I would eventually work after achieving my degrees. The person I was afraid to talk to was the person I would eventually become.)

So I handled it the only way I believed I could — on my own. That college catalog became my bible. My goal was to enter Suffolk County Community College in September, and I had three months to figure out how to get started and what I wanted to study.

At that point, I didn't have a clue about what I wanted to be, or do with my life. I just knew I wanted to be educated so I could earn a decent income and feel good about myself. I remember thinking that I didn't want to just go out and get a job at the neighborhood store making five dollars an hour. I wanted more than that for myself, both financially and academically; I felt I was worth more. I believed in my ability, but I was still scared to death of getting started. So there I was, pouring through the pages of a book I had no previous familiarity with, a book that held the key to my future — whatever that was.

I read and I read, and I studied each and every program offered at the college. Some could be instantly ruled out. I had no interest in nursing; although the money was good, it was not something I could see myself handling. I didn't have the stomach for anything in the medical field. There were numerous degree programs in business and computers. There was theater, and music, and art, and criminal justice, none of which were for me. Paralegal looked interesting, as did photography. I enjoyed decorating and, there was a degree for interior design. I liked fashion but there was nothing in that area, only business courses that prepared one for continued study at colleges like FIT or Parson's School of Design. I couldn't think that far ahead. The choices seemed endless and dizzying for me, a person with no clue and no experience in anything but caring for children. But I knew I had to start somewhere, so I decided to take a different approach to this undertaking. I would read each degree program again to determine which course or courses were required in every program. That would allow me the time needed to know what the right choices were for me.

It was critical that I made my decision wisely, as I had neither the time nor the money to waste at this stage of my busy life. I was already feeling a little selfish for wanting to spend money on myself for the tuition it would cost. So for the next couple of days I devoted all of my free time to the task of course selection. Some mornings would find me settled in at the kitchen counter with my coffee and my course catalog before the sun, or the children had risen. I'd begin by determining which courses were required in a majority of the programs, then I'd read the description to decide whether this was a course that would hold my interest and would be one that I believed I could handle. Morning after morning, before the house came alive, night after night, after the quiet settled in, my ritual persisted until I'd figured it out. There appeared to be two courses that were required in just about every degree program — Freshman Composition Writing and Psychology. It was settled; I'd decided on my first two courses. I was going to college! And I was still terrified and still insecure, but I wanted it more than I was afraid of it so I knew I had to keep going.

I remember watching an episode of "The Voice," where a judge, Pharrell Williams, gave inspiring advice to one of his contestants that lost. He said: "Keep going! If you stop now, then "no" is right." That's what I did, and that's what you will need to do too.

Right now you are one choice away from a new beginning - one that leads you toward becoming the fullest human being you can be.

Oprah Winfrey

Chapter 8

Stepping Slowly through the College Doors

Dinner was cleared away. The children were all taken care of, and I was feeling sick to my stomach. *You can do this,* I told myself, over and over. *But I'm 39, and I'll be the oldest student in class.* Try as I might, I couldn't shake the fear. I summoned up every motivational quote I could think of. I replayed Abby's advice over and over in my mind. *Wouldn't you rather look back and say, I did it? Yes, I would,* I thought. *That's why I have to go through with this.* But it didn't ease the sick feeling that would stay with me through the entire class session.

So with pen and pad in hand, I entered my first class, English 101 and took a seat in the second row near the door. To the left of me sat, what looked like to be, an 18-year-old boy staring at the blank desk in front of him, like he was ready to nod off. To the right of me sat another 18-year-old, leaning back with his feet on the chair in front of him. My typical motherly instinct could only concentrate on the furniture he was defacing with his feet. I wondered if his parent had ever taught him the proper way to sit on other people's furniture. But of course, those inner thoughts remained inside as I tried to remind myself that in this atmosphere, at this time, I was a student, not a mother, not a homemaker, but a student like everyone else in the room. Looking around the room, it was hard not to feel out of place. In every seat was a young adult, none older than 19. Some of them didn't look older than 16. At least that's how it appeared to me. I kept thinking that I was old enough to be their mother. At age 39, I definitely was old enough and probably older than some of their mothers. I felt one of my biggest fears was materializing. I was too old for this. I imagined everyone looking at me and thinking they were in class with their mother. It was so difficult to focus, yet I felt safer just sitting in my seat quietly. Even if I wanted to stand up and run out of there, I was frozen in my seat.

As I continued to be absorbed in my lack of self-confidence, the door opened, and in walked an older gentleman who introduced himself as Professor Charles. *Well, that's a relief,* I thought, *another older person.* Of course, he was probably in his mid-thirties, but at least he wasn't part of the "just out of high school crowd." He went right to the board and began writing our first assignment that was due the following week. This was reinforced in the six page syllabus that followed. I took a deep breath and thought, *I can do this. That's what I'm here for.* But the sick feeling was still there, and at that moment, I still didn't really believe that I could do it.

So I sat frozen in my seat as the professor called attendance and went through every line of the syllabus. When I wasn't diligently taking notes, I was noticing that few others around me were writing at all. I've never understood how students could get by without taking notes. Even now, as I stand on the other side of the desk, looking out at my students in front of me, I am amazed at how few take notes. Interestingly, it is still the older adult students who write as diligently as I did on that first night of class.

An hour and a half into class, the teacher announced a break and instructed us to be back in our seats 15 minutes later. I watched as the others filed out to have a smoke, or get a snack from the machines downstairs. Some remained in their seat and laid their heads down on the marked up, dirty desks. I just sat there - people watching and wondering what I was doing there. The professor paused and asked, "Any questions?" I could think of one or two questions to ask but of course I was wary of having everyone looking at me. As I contemplated asking my question, I wondered, *What if I asked a stupid question? What if it was something obvious that I should know the answer to?* Then, as if he could hear my thoughts, the professor loudly said to the class, "There are no bad or stupid questions; if you thought of something that was unclear to you, chances are that someone else is puzzled by the same thing. Do not hesitate or feel embarrassed to ask a question because I strongly welcome it." Then he added:

"However, one thing I will not entertain is students waiting until the end of class to ask their questions. In other words, do not come up to me after I've dismissed class to ask your question, because, like you, I expect to leave when class is ended and not hang around to answer questions that should have been asked during class time. I will stop whatever I am doing to answer your questions in class and I will take as much time as needed to clear up any confusion, but I will not take the time after class."

He made his point loud and clear, and we all got his message, especially when he pointed out that, like us, he wanted to be out of there at the end of class. Those words still resonate with me today when I'm standing in front of my own students repeating the same message I heard on that first night of my college career. The point here is you should not hesitate to ask questions. If you are confused, chances are others are as well, and you will only stress over it later.

An hour later, I was back in my car heading for the safety of home. By then, my head ached in unison with my stomach. All I wanted to do was get under the covers and feel secure again. I told myself it would be better in the morning. I told myself I could do this. I had to do this if I was going to make something of myself. I couldn't neglect my education now that I had committed to it. But still, I wondered, why did it have to be so hard?

Later, I replayed Abby's message over and over in my head as I tried to fall off to sleep. *In 10 years you'll be 45 . . . wouldn't you rather look back and say, I did it. Yes, I would,* I answered to myself. *I want to be able to say I did it!* With those positive thoughts, I fell asleep.

Prepare yourself; it's going to be hard, and it's going to be painful at times, and you're going to feel defeated at times. I felt all those things over and over, as you can see, even from day one of my journey, and it would be a long one, but I kept at it. I looked for the inspiration wherever I could find it. I held on to it, and then I sought out more because for every encouragement I encountered, there was always more discouragement coming at me.

Mary Tyler Moore tells us: "Take chances, make mistakes. That's how you grow. Pain nourishes your courage. You have to fail in order to practice being brave." I don't know why that is true, I just know it is. So, believe it and allow it to nourish your courage to succeed.

Never discourage anyone . . . who continually makes progress, no matter how slow. The learning and knowledge that we have, is, at the most, but little compared with that of which we are ignorant.

Plato

Chapter 9

Gathering Support

The warm, bright light that targeted my face served as my alarm clock in the morning. The night before was a blur. My first waking thoughts imagined it was all a dream, but slowly, the recollection returned, and the details began to unfold. I wondered if it was really as bad as I had made it out to be. *Maybe not*, I hoped. Then the fear began to creep back, and I thought, *God I hope I took good notes!* Of course I did, but there was that insecurity creeping in again.

I had two hours before the kids would be up. Dave was already off to work, and it was too early to call either of my sisters. Karen is a morning person, but five o'clock was a little too early for conversation, and it was hours too early to call Cathy. I wanted to talk to someone, to tell someone all about my first class. Even if they didn't understand why I was putting myself through this, I knew they would listen.

Like most people who'd heard of my plan to attend college at almost 40 years old, Karen had expressed her doubts initially.

"Isn't that going to take a long time to finish? How old are you going to be when you're done?"

"Around 45," I responded.

"And you're going to look for a job at that age?"

"45 is not old, I can do this," I responded less convincingly.

"I have no doubts that you can do it; it just seems like a lot of work and a lot of time, but you should go for it if that's what you want." Karen would never try to talk me out of something I'd planned to do, even if she didn't understand it. She had confidence in my choices, and she often looked to me for guidance in her own choices in life.

Karen

***

At 10 years younger than me, with a husband and three young daughters close in age, Karen often felt overwhelmed by her busy life. The gym became her place to work out her frustrations. Before long, she was crafting her own routines and training others in her home gym. We'd often talk about her aspirations to do more with her talent for fitness, but when you're 29, with three little ones depending on you, it's difficult to envision life beyond the confines of the home and family.

As my credits began to accumulate, and progress was becoming more evident, our conversations would include possible ways for Karen to progress in her field. With three young daughters, ages two, four and nine, college wasn't an option, so she made the decision to expand her knowledge and her skills through self-study. Recently, I asked Karen to recall how she got started.

"I began through online research and talking to other fitness specialists. This helped guide me in the right direction. There were books to buy, and practice tests to master, and workshops to attend. Keep in mind; I was never a serious student in high school, so this was like starting over for me. I had to fit in an hour or two of studying as early as 4:30 before the family was awake and again after they went to bed. Then, just as I was preparing for my certification exams, I became pregnant, and plans had to be put on hold." That would only be the first of many changes Karen would have to adapt to, each strengthening her resolve.

After the birth of her son, Karen was able to complete her practical and written exams and begin working three days a week at the local Gold's Gym in the afternoons when her husband was home with the kids.

"Was it hard to pick up where you left off after Michael was born?" I asked.

"The time just seemed to fly back then. As soon as I'd get the girls off to school, I would begin working with clients who I had scheduled for personal training. I always made sure to leave time for my own workouts, and of course, I still had a baby to care for. In the afternoons, I would get the homework started while preparing dinner, pack something for myself and leave for my job at the gym as soon as my husband got home. This continued until all the children were in school, and I could accept a part-time job in Manhattan as a trainer for American Express."

What seemed an ideal situation, allowing Karen to manage family and a great job, would once again change. In 2001, the American Express building was one of many damaged by the attack on the World Trade Center causing Karen to lose her job. Of course, as she concurred, this was a small price to pay compared to so many others who had lost so much more.

"What was that like for you?" I asked.

"Well, even though it was a part-time job, it was tough. I still had clients that I trained at home but so many others lost their livelihood. I began looking into benefits I might be eligible for and learned I could receive reimbursement for yoga instructor training. That interested me, but it would involve months of studying that ended in a four day required retreat in Virginia."

Karen knew this was right for her, and she would make it work. The training took place three days a week at a school in the city which was more manageable than the required studying. As she explained, "I had to take courses in Anatomy and Physiology. It was insane! It was like learning another language! But I got through it, and I have no regrets." Like many of us, Karen agreed that her hard work and sacrifices were worth the satisfying career she has gained.

Cathy
✳✳✳

Cathy was surprised at my choice but understood my aspiration. "I'm really proud of you sis." She, too, saw the long road ahead of me but respected my judgment and believed in my abilities. When Cathy graduated high school after only three years, she fought to be able to attend college, but our father saw no importance in further education and insisted she find a job. But just any job was not good enough for Cathy. She was determined to use everything she learned as an honor student in high school to impress the employers, and it worked. In no time, Cathy was hired at a major investment brokerage firm in Manhattan at a higher pay than was originally advertised. There she learned all she could before being swayed to join another major financial corporation.

Cathy was never satisfied with the status quo. She took every opportunity to educate herself in all aspects of business. When marriage and children required her to leave the corporate world, Cathy applied her acquired business expertise to a new venture that would allow her to be both entrepreneur and homemaker. As she explained:

"I loved being a parent, but I knew I could be using more of my skills and talents to contribute to the household financially. At the time, DVR and Netflix didn't exist. All we had were video rentals so the idea of owning a video store seemed perfect."

"I vaguely remember that. How did you manage to afford it?" I inquired.

"Well, I partnered with my brother-in-law for the initial investment but I essentially ran the business. Sometimes he would come in and try to make decisions for me rather than in consultation, but I wouldn't tolerate it." She continued, "I remember this one time he showed up with an expensive glass showcase he had purchased on his own, and I made him return it. If we were going to be partners, I told him, we needed to make all decisions together. That was a big frustration for me because I knew my capabilities but I was never treated as an equal."

I listened to her account with admiration and then inquired, "Who took care of the children while you were at the store?"

"I took them with me. We had a room in the back that I turned into a playroom. The boys were four and seven and Tricia was ten. When they weren't in school or activities, they were playing or doing their homework right there.

I made it work but it wasn't easy. When one of them was sick, I'd have to scramble to get someone to open up the store. After my work day was done at the store, a new workday would begin at home with dinner to prepare and homework to check, baths and bedtime. Plus I was getting four of us ready for work the next day. Often in the evenings, there were business calls to address. This was another source of stress and conflict as my husband demanded my full attention, and refused to see that I was making every effort to balance home and children and a business. Still, I continued to make it work while the children were young and dependent on me. Having this personal accomplishment also reinforced a much desired belief in my own abilities."

I admired Cathy's fortitude. Throughout her adult life she would often be put in positions to stand up for herself and for what was fair. As her children grew in age and independence, Cathy pursued other ventures. As she explained,

"I began to want something that would help me grow professionally, and I needed to sever the partnership that existed in name only. In my first part-time position, the cycle would repeat itself. As an office manager, the head doctor recognized my potential and dedication and as a result, delved out excessive responsibility that would never match the salary he was willing to pay. While the job provided me with increased business experience and knowledge, it lacked the self-respect I needed and deserved. Knowing that I would never get far with him, I began seeking other positions."

Cathy's determination prevailed, and before long, she was an upper management administrator in a large MRI company where she was appreciated both professionally and financially. Cathy's challenges didn't end there.

One of her major trials came after she'd turned 50, with a decision she had been contemplating for years. Cathy's aspiration was to move to Florida and start a new life. She knew she couldn't uproot her children so she kept putting her dream aside, waiting for the right time. We all know that the right time can often be interrupted by life's events, and this was no different for Cathy. There were marriages and births and of course, lack of understanding from the kids, not to mention the cynics who thought she was as crazy as me for wanting to take on such a life changing endeavor at this stage of her life. Still, she held on to her dream that one day she would make that move, and one day she did. I asked Cathy to talk about the difficulties she faced getting to that point. She had this to say:

"I had to pull from every ounce of strength that I had and curb living for everyone else. There were a lot of tears and a lot of guilt. I spent a lot of time wondering if I was doing the right thing. My friends would add salt to the wounds by saying things like, 'How can you leave your kids?' People thought I was selfish."

"How did your children react?" I asked.

"They were all adults by then. Thomas was 19 and Michael 22 so the boys saw it as a place to visit. Tricia, on the other hand, was devastated, but between us, we continue to have frequent visits and daily phone calls."

The thought of moving can intimidate the best of us, but moving states away with little more than the clothes on her back, leaving family and friends behind, is unfathomable to me. But once her decision was made, there was no looking back. There was a house to sell and garage sales to help get rid of the contents. Dan had to relocate with his job while Cathy quit hers. They had to find temporary accommodations in Florida that would accept their two dogs.

Before long, everything was in place, and we were wishing them well as they made the drive south. Recently, I asked Cathy how she got through it in the face of so much opposition. She had this to say:

"I wanted it more than I was afraid."

Ellie

***

Others were totally perplexed by my decision, like my sister-in-law, Ellie, who responded to my announcement as we sat on her steps, one afternoon, catching up.

"You're going to start college at this stage of your life? Really? Aren't you nervous about taking on such a big venture? I could never do it."

"Sure I'm nervous, but I want to do this for myself, and I think I can." I replied.

"Well, I give you credit. I hope you do well; I couldn't do it." She reiterated.

The words of acceptance were being said, but I knew Ellie didn't understand why I wanted to bring all this on myself. We were raised similarly to want the same things in life. Girls were expected to grow into women who got married and had children and became good wives and mothers, and there was nothing wrong with that expectation. I welcomed that ideology my entire life. I longed for the day that I would marry and become like my own mom — a housewife and mother. It's what I wanted then and what I still respected even as I sought to step outside of its doors. So even if Ellie didn't identify with my choices, she could listen and accept them because they were my choices. From time to time, she would ask how things were going and would always express her pride in my efforts and accomplishments.

As our conversation continued, I reminded Ellie that she, too, was able to overcome some challenges when she was my age.

"What challenges?" She asked. "I've never gone to college. I have no interest."

"No, but you adapted to a major move; you learned how to drive; you got a job and learned how to use a computer, all while in your 40s and 50s. Ellie, these are all major accomplishments! How did it feel when you were going through all of these changes? Was it easy? Were there times when you didn't think you could get through it?" I persisted.

Ellie listened pensively then added, "It's true; the move from the Bronx was the blackest day of my life. I was actually hoping we wouldn't get approved for the mortgage." Her voice got serious as she continued to recall this time in her life.

"I was born and raised in the same building, so leaving it at 37 was tough. But the hardest part of the move was leaving my

61

mother. My father died in March and by October, I was moving. I hated leaving her, but she never complained. It took a few months to adjust to the change; until then, I couldn't stop crying"

Ellie's words reminded me of my own experience. "I can relate, Ellie. I remember kissing my mom and getting in the car for the drive to our new home on Long Island. The entire trip was spent in silence as I stared out the window with tears streaming down my face. I felt bad for Dave, but he understood."

Ellie continued to recall the move from the Bronx where life was so different from what she found waiting for her in the suburbs. For the families in that tenement community, anything they needed was only steps away. Friends were at the doorstep for children and parents. If you ran out of bread or milk, you could send your child down the block to the grocery store. When more groceries were needed, you would take along a two-wheeled shopping cart, fill it up and wheel it home.

Conversely, life in the suburbs was less carefree, and for the most part, required a car to get around. Women had to drive their children to play dates, and if you ran out of milk or bread, there was no grocery store within walking distance. In the city, there was never a need for a second car, thus, there was never a need for Ellie to know how to drive.

"In the beginning, I made the attempt to walk to stores. It wasn't ideal but I needed to retain some of my independence."

With few friends in her new neighborhood, Ellie needed more to fill her time now that her own children were becoming more independent. The thought of working outside the home after all these years was daunting for her. As she put it,

"I was petrified! After 17 years as a stay at home parent, the thought of being in a whole new world of unfamiliar territory was frightening."

Now, learning to drive was imperative. It was a stressful undertaking, but once accomplished, it afforded Ellie a much needed, newfound freedom. Her new job in an ENT office brought challenges of learning that were both intimidating and rewarding.

Not unlike the experiences of most of us, there were days when Ellie wished for her old life back and days when she just felt too old for the new trials she faced every day. Of course she was not too old at the young age of forty-something, still the intricate tasks required of her sometimes seemed too much to handle. There were computer programs to master followed by new, updated computer programs to master again. But Ellie stuck with it, and when the work was not satisfying, the social atmosphere of the job filled the void.

The challenges that face many adults are not always centered on the tests of formal education. Like Ellie, my mom was faced with a life changing move.

Connie

***

After residing for twenty-five years, and raising five children in one section of Brooklyn, where stores, school, doctor and church were within a couple of blocks, a move to a more isolated neighborhood, made it immediately evident to my mom that very little was in walking distance. So, at the age of 52 years young, Connie found herself studying a manual and taking practice tests to earn her driver's permit. This was not an easy task for someone who had been out of school for more than 30 years, someone who went from high school to working as a seamstress. Still, in a few short months and a lot of hours of studying, Connie earned her driver's permit and could begin practicing behind the wheel.

Getting behind the wheel of a car for the first time was another tremendous feat. With determination and motivation guiding her, she enrolled with a professional driving school and practiced what she learned with her son-in-law, my husband, Dave. In less than a year, my mom attained her driver's license and soon became the neighborhood driver of all her women friends. What may not seem like a great accomplishment for some, was huge for a homemaker of more than twenty-five years who never had to open up a book to study. Thus, it took a lot for her to complete such a task at that stage of her life. Connie had to forget her age and believe that she could do this for herself. It took a lot of determination, but her hard work, and ultimate success, served as a positive reinforcement for all of us.

My mom and sisters and sisters-in-laws could always be counted on for support. They were each going through their own life changes, and I was always available to listen to them. We often leaned on each other when life got heavy with responsibility. Each of them achieved their own success in various ways, epitomizing my mantra, "Forget your age, you can do this!"

More Sources of Support

***

Having people in your life who will listen and support you is of the utmost importance on the road to success. Who will your support system be? If you're lucky, it can start with your spouse. However, you shouldn't be upset if that isn't the case. Realize that not everyone can turn to a husband or a wife or partner for support. Not all spouses are capable or willing to share their partner's new endeavors. Some may feel threatened by the new interests that they see as coming between them.

I was fortunate to have a husband who understood what it meant for me to have goals and aspirations of my own. Dave recognized that I needed to experience self-fulfillment. At times, it wasn't easy for him; in fact, often, it took a tremendous amount of patience and endurance. Still, it was helpful to have my support system begin at home. If that is not the best situation for you, find another source of support. Maybe you have a good friend who can be that person for you or maybe a sister or a brother who is willing to listen and offer encouragement.

Another good source of support can be your own children. Many adult students are old enough, as I was, to have grown children in college. Sharing experiences with them can provide a whole new level of connectedness between parent and child. Most children are proud of the parent who puts themselves through college or starts a new endeavor. It's kind of a "practice what you preach" situation. We preach the importance of college to our children. We preach the importance of commitment and reaching goals and now we can show them how much we believe in the importance of these values.

My daughter was in her first year of college at Stony Brook University when I was ready to move up to the university from the community college. Jenn was a great help in my attempt to navigate the vast grounds of my new surroundings. Her natural love of literature inspired me to take on courses that I would usually avoid. Authors like Dante and Shakespeare, who I would normally find intimidating, now appealed to me. Knowing I could share the experience with my daughter, and I could tap into her expertise on these fascinating writers, made the experience that much more enjoyable and meaningful.

Later in my academic journey, both my sons were attending college. Not only could they now appreciate my struggles first hand, but Dave and Dan and I could now become a mutual support system to each other. Having gone through the community college and the university system, they accepted my advice on courses, instructors and who to talk to for answers. And, like their sister, Dave and Dan would sometimes engage in conversations with me about academic issues. This, in itself, served as positive reinforcement for my own experiences. Even as an adult married man, Dan continues to remind me of some of the same advice I shared with him over the years and listen patiently when I need to discuss my writing or classwork.

You need to accept the support wherever you can find it because for every person who is there for you, you will encounter as many naysayers, skeptics and pessimists. There will be those who try to discourage you, those who will make you question your choices; even those who will offer you advice on how to do it better. Naysayers promote negativity. They will make you feel like it can't be done.

I encountered many on my path to success. Someone once told me I was crazy to be pursuing this at my age and it would be "a hell of a lot easier to just go out and get a job and work my way up the ladder." I was 40 at the time, with no experience and no training. Had I listened to her advice, I'd still be working my way up a very short ladder with no college degree. Rather than let these people influence my decisions, I used their words to fuel my fire and worked harder to reach my goals.

You need to stay focused and ignore the cynics. Believe that there is no room in your life for negativity. Believe in yourself and your abilities to succeed. Trust your judgment when doubts get in the way and work harder. Heed the wise words of Winston Churchill, who said: "Continuous effort, not strength or intelligence, is the key to unlocking our potential. Difficulties mastered are opportunities won. Courage is what it takes to stand up and speak. Courage is also what it takes to sit down and listen." Sometimes, we have no choice but to listen to the advice that is imparted to us, good or bad; however, we have the choice to let our actions speak for our words.

Another personal favorite to recall when confronted by naysayers is this quote from Friedrich Nietzsche: ". . . and those who were seen dancing were thought to be insane by those who could not hear the music." Ponder that for a moment.

I get by with a little help from my friends.

John Lennon

Chapter 10

Adding to the Support System

Regardless of how large or small your support system is, there will always be times when you will feel completely alone and times when you will have no one but yourself to rely on. That morning after my first class was one of those situations for me.

As I read over the syllabus, most of the general information was familiar. I knew the attendance policy and was not too concerned about missing class; even my fear wouldn't keep me from class. It was the assignment section that I was interested in. Three pages listed by date for the next fifteen weeks. I looked at what was due for next class: Read pages 1-25 in the text. Write a one page paper on the poem, "My Papa's Waltz" and one for each of the three Norman Rockwell paintings on pages 26-28. *Is he kidding?* I thought. *Twenty eight pages of reading and four pages of writing - and this is just the first assignment! I know I have a week to get this done, but I'll be up all night, every night this week!* Just then a thought occurred to me. *Damn, I never bought the book!* I was in such a hurry to get home that I didn't think to go to the bookstore. Now I was in a panic. There was nothing I could do. I'd go back to the college as soon as the kids were off to school. *What a waste of valuable time,* I thought.

Three hours later, I was standing on the outside of the student center trying to corral three kids for as long as it would take to reach my destination, located inside the building ahead of us, down the stairs and around the corner. Fortunately, the other students were both enamored and entertained by my little entourage. It quickly became evident that the line, not unlike those in other venues, turned into its own social network. Students began chatting with those in front or behind them. Snacks were shared; names were exchanged and friendships were being formed. One young woman who had befriended my son, Danny, turned to me and asked:

"So what classes are you taking?"

"Freshman Comp and Psychology," I responded.

"Oh, good choices; who's the professor?"

"Um, Professor Charles for English Composition and I don't know who my psychology teacher is; that class hasn't met yet."

"Oh, Professor Charles?" she replied with a degree of ambiguity.

"Do you know him?" I inquired.

"Actually, I had him for that same class last semester,"

"Really? What did you think?"

"Well, if I can be honest, he's tough, but fair. He'll make you work, but you'll learn the essentials of good writing if you can keep up with the work."

"Keeping up with the work is exactly what worries me. On the first night of class, he assigned four pages of writing and 28 pages of reading. I haven't been in school for 25 years. I'm just not sure . . ."

"Listen," she interrupted, "what you need to do is not let it overwhelm you. Take it one week at a time and follow his instructions. Ask for clarification if you're not sure of something; he loves that. He'd rather stop the class and answer questions than let you be confused. Did he tell you he doesn't answer questions at the end of class?

"Yes, why does he do that?" I asked. "I'd feel better waiting until after class to ask my questions."

"Well, that's his way of getting everyone to start feeling comfortable talking in class. Plus, he's not answering the same questions over and over if the students ask them in front of each other. Did he tell you about the public speaking assignment yet?"

"What?" I retorted.

She laughed at my reaction. "It's really not that bad; everyone takes a turn each week summarizing one of the readings and asking a couple of questions related to the writing of that particular text."

"So, I have to get up in front of the class?"

"No, don't worry," she answered amusingly. "You just sit at your desk and talk to the class in a circle."

"Oh, we have to sit in a circle?" I inquired.

"He hasn't had you do that yet?" She asked. "That's probably because it was the first class, but, he will. By the way, what's your name?"

"It's Chris, what's yours?"

"Marsha, your kids are cute. You'll have your hands full between them and coursework," she observed.

"Actually, only one is mine. Danny is my son, and I take care of the two girls for my friend but I do have another son, David, and a daughter, Jennifer who are both in school."

"Wow, you really do have your hands full. Where do you find the motivation, not to mention the time?"

"I'm not sure. That's why I'm so afraid. I have the determination, but I keep questioning myself about my ability . . ."

Marsha interrupted again. "Listen, you have to keep believing in yourself if this is something you really want to do. Here, take my number; sometimes, I get insecure too. We can get together and help each other out."

"Really?" I smiled. "Thanks, I'd like that."

The bookstore entrance was now in sight. The wait seemed to go quickly, spent talking with my newfound friend. I learned that Marsha was also in her late thirties with three children of her own. Like me, she was a returning adult student with family responsibilities. Once inside, we went our separate ways reiterating that we would stay in touch. With my three troopers following behind, I lugged my textbooks to the car and headed home to begin the serious business of college work.

Later, I recalled my conversation with Marsha. I'd hoped she wasn't just speaking out of politeness. I could really use a supportive friend right now. I thought about a quote by Oprah Winfrey, who said: "Surround yourself only with people who are going to lift you higher." It seemed to make so much sense to me at that moment. It's what we all must do as we strive to succeed.

There are no secrets to success. It is the result of preparation, hard work and learning from failure.

Colin Powell

Chapter 11

Finding Your Space

So, you register, you attend your first class, buy your books and find the motivation to get to work. Then, looking down at everything laid out before you, you think, *where do I begin?* An important first step is to find your comfort zone. Find a place where you can work and study comfortably. It should not be so comfortable that you may be easily distracted or tempted to nod off. It should not be a place where your daily undertakings are normally accomplished. Your new comfort zone should be a place that you go to solely for the purpose of completing your academic work.

Where will your work space be? Some choose to seek the quiet of the library to study and read, a perfectly sensible choice if one can afford the time away from home. However, most adult students tend to go from work, to class, to car, to home or from home, to class, to home. Most only see the inside of the library out of necessity for research. Nevertheless, for those fortunate to have the time to spend on campus, the library can provide the space needed for serious study.

***

For most adult students, time is as important as the task itself. Whether you're a homemaker or a businessman or woman commuting from work, all are working to find the best and quickest method to succeed at their new mission. More time spent outside the home is not an option, and necessity may dictate the workspace. For me, it was my kitchen counter. It was not the ideal space, but I made it work. Most of my study time had to be shared with the family TV time, in the next room. It was as frustrating for the family as it was for me. Concentrating was impossible at times and asking three kids and their dad to lower the volume only exposed the level of laughter and talking among them. As I had to learn, it quickly becomes necessary to block it out and try to work around the noise. Realize that the other members in your household must be expected to continue their daily routines just as you must be expected to follow your newly acquired one. If this absolutely will not work, you may have to adjust your life in other areas. You might get up early and get in some study time before everyone is awake or stay up later at night after everyone else is asleep. Keep in mind that the greatest sacrificing will need to come from you.

I have always been a morning person, never one to stay up very late. Once I started to take night classes, that all changed. I would get home from school feeling exhausted but unable to sleep right away. So, after a snack and a little mindless television, I would get some of my assignments started. There were also nights when I could not look at another book, and the mindless television was all I could handle. Find what works for you, and steal the time whenever you can.

Some nights I would stare at the digital numbers on my clock radio waiting for sleep to come. When it didn't, I found it more productive to go into the kitchen and read or write until my eyes grew heavy. Other times I would awaken at four in the morning feeling invigorated so I'd get in a chapter of reading before the sun came up. You need to do whatever it takes to insure success.

If the house gets too noisy at night, try taking your work to the neighborhood bookstore, grab a cup of coffee and a table or a couch, and spend an hour concentrating on the subject at hand. You'll be surprised at how much can be accomplished in a short time. You might feel like you are doing something for yourself in a social sense as well.

***

It is imperative that your new undertaking be accomplished in the least stressful atmosphere possible. I will not preach unrealistic expectations to you; we know that stress will be difficult to avoid at times. If you find yourself weighed down with work at home, at school and after school, you will begin to lose interest, and that is what you want to avoid at all costs. So how do you do that?

I certainly will not imply that you should increase your social life because that is the first thing to go when taking on any new endeavor. Instead, try to infuse small moments of variety into your schoolwork schedule that will allow you to accomplish the task at hand while feeling like you are also doing something thoughtful for yourself. Let's get specific.

When I was attending Stony Brook University, my classes often followed a hectic day of running from home to student teaching. That was sometimes followed by after-school activities and meetings, then on to work and, afterwards, to school. Add to that the early morning laundry and lunch preparation. (See, I told you my life was like yours!) Once on campus, I needed to unwind and get into learning mode. I discovered an area just outside one of the academic buildings where one could feel totally alone in the midst of hundreds of people. The small section held a concrete wading pool with trickling water, shaded by a huge tree that dripped its leaves into the water. Sitting on the edge of that pool made me feel like I had been transported to the tranquil area of Provence in the south of France. It came to feel like my own private sanctuary where I could go after a frenzied day and before a demanding evening in class. Many productive hours were spent reading and studying in my newfound haven, leaving me refreshed and ready to tackle another class.

Perhaps your haven can be a patch of grass under a tree on campus or outside of work; or you can find a bench somewhere under the warm sun or the shaded branches; bring your lunch or a snack, open up your book, and get to work. It doesn't have to be a quiet place with no one around. Some afternoons, I preferred the openness of a bench near the sprawling fountain in the middle of campus with people rushing back and forth. If the space makes you feel relaxed, it will be easy to block out the world around you. The important thing is to feel good in whatever space you choose. If you try, you can find beauty in most anything and turn it into something special for you. Use your imagination. My special place was nothing more than an old hole in the ground with a couple of inches of water, cluttered with leaves. That certainly does not sound like the spot I described above, nor is it as poetic. It is simply another example of our mind's ability to attain. I liken it to a quote spoken by Milton, who said, "The mind is its own place, and in itself, can make heaven of Hell, a hell of Heaven."

From a certain point onward there is no longer any turning back.
That is the point that must be reached.

Franz Kafka

Chapter 12

How to Afford Your New Venture

I'm sure the financial concern has entered your mind and has been one of the many things preventing many of you from getting started. Financial concern is valid. You need to know how you will pay for your new undertaking. If you are serious about reaching your goal, you need to figure out a way to make it happen. Therefore, your research and exploration must include financial planning.

The one thing you should not do is assume that you cannot afford to see your dream through to completion and give up. As Kafka said, "you must reach the point where you will no longer turn back." To this I add, that point should be the moment you make up your mind to realize your dream.

Yes, that is easier said than done. It was difficult for me, as well, to keep from turning back, but I had already begun to believe that this was a now-or-never situation. If I couldn't find a way to do this now, I would never be able to do it later. If I couldn't afford it now, I would not be able to afford it a year from now. Keep in mind, expenses do not usually lessen, they only change. In other words, what you spend on the family now, you will still be spending later, but it will be on different things.

In my case, we had three children across a span of ten years. As each child outgrew diapers and formula, there was another to take the place. Then there were new expenses of baby food, organic milk and training underwear to replace the diapers and formula of the previous child. Fast forward to when all three children were out of diapers, formula, baby food and so on; now we had three more mouths to feed for the rest of the time our children lived with us. As you know, that can be years and years. Our youngest son did not move out until he was 28.

That is just a natural part of life, and we would not want it any other way. Of course, the scenario differs in every family, but the reality is that our lives are not solely our own, and we have to find ways to work around this fact and not see it as something getting in the way of our success or use it as an excuse to keep from getting started.

So, how would you do that? Well, don't worry; you don't have to take food out of your children's mouths - in case that is what you are thinking. For those of you who think I am being sarcastic, I am absolutely serious. I have had many adults, both men and women, sit in front of me and say that they don't see how they can afford to go to college at the expense of their children's needs. My advice to all who share this concern is to start at the logical place, right at the college, in the financial aid office.

Financial aid has far too many specifications to elaborate on, so I am not about to begin listing the variables on these pages. What I recommend is that you just apply. It is the standard rule of thumb that every student should fill out the necessary paperwork to determine eligibility for funding. Do not assume that you will not qualify. Even those who are not eligible for aid can qualify for student loans. Keep in mind: you should go through your college for any kind of government assistance, not a bank or an agent. Your college will afford you the best rates and the best payback plans. However, you must be enrolled in a degree program in order to qualify for this aid.

You can also search the web for colleges throughout the country that offer tuition breaks. Visit sites like Yahoo Finance (finance.yahoo.com) where careful research will reveal some who offer free tuition to students just for being accepted. Like everything else, you must do the research. There are other websites that provide a wealth of information, far too many than I can list here. One that immediately comes to mind is finaid.org, a free public service guide.

For those of you already in full time employment, paying for college may be as easy as knowing your own benefit package. Many companies and agencies offer tuition reimbursement. Some may require certain guidelines for your course of study. Others may stipulate certain courses for promotion. Unless you desire to completely change your career, tuition reimbursement is a worthwhile benefit to explore.

Not to be overlooked are veteran's benefits. Those of you who have given so much in service to your country should not hesitate to seek reimbursement for college tuition. It can be as simple as providing your release papers or DD214 to your college registrar.

My husband Dave, a veteran of Vietnam, utilized these benefits to enroll in courses for promotion. We had just purchased our first home and had our first child so affording this new undertaking was a concern. Taking courses would earn him more money, which was an important consideration given our new financial obligations. Fortunately, Dave sought and received guidance through his job and college in time to take advantage of tuition reimbursement through the Veteran's Association.

What he didn't expect was the added convenience of being able to take all of his classes right in the precinct house. Dave explained:

"At the time, a college degree was not a requirement for police officers and once we were on the job, it was difficult to fit courses in with our different shifts." As he spoke, I was reminded of Dave's varied schedules throughout the years. At times he worked from four to midnight, and at other times, his work hours began at midnight and ended at eight in the morning. Anyone would have difficulty working around those shifts, I thought as Dave continued:

"While I was looking for information about the VA benefits, I learned about a program called CAPP. This was an accredited college degree program through NYIT for police officers. All of the officers who enrolled in CAPP, or New York Institute of Technology's College Accelerated Program for Police, were veterans who were able to take advantage of tuition reimbursement."

"How, exactly, did this program work? What made it successful?" I asked.

"It worked because it allowed officers, like me, to earn college credits while working on the job. There was an agreement between the college and the police department that allowed professors from NYIT to teach in our precinct station houses. This worked out well when I had to be on call or go to court because we were enrolled in the same courses and could catch up on any work that we missed."

"I remember it being overwhelming at times," I added.

"It was; especially when I needed to write papers or study for tests. By then, I had been out of school for some time and had the added responsibilities of a family and a full-time job that often went into overtime. Still, the convenience of having the professors come to our workplace was a big help."

"Was it worth the time and effort for you?" I asked.

"It was worth it. Taking college courses allowed me to move forward more quickly and earn more money. Later on, the credits were necessary for my promotion to sergeant. Also, the tuition benefit through the Veterans' Association was a great financial help. Everyone who has the option to receive this benefit should take advantage of it."

Dave made a good point and this advice should be heeded. To that I would reiterate the importance of research. You need to ask questions and learn about the opportunities that are available to you. Every place of employment will have different options with different criteria, but one might be just the right fit for you. Remember that financial consideration is important if you are to reach that point referred to by Kafka.

***

Aside from government aid and employee benefits, there are myriad ways to afford paying for college tuition. Here is where you need to look at your own life and get creative. Where do you begin? How about starting with costly vices? We all have them, some more than others. For instance, do you smoke? Do you drink, whether regularly or occasionally? Are you aware of how much either or both of these practices are costing you weekly, monthly, annually? Let's do the math. Since cigarettes are easiest to calculate, I will start there. Assuming you are not purchasing your cigarettes illegally, you are probably paying about $8.00 a pack. I will use that as the average since the price is as high as $14.50 a pack in places like New York City. So, if you smoke a pack a day, that's $56.00 per week, $240.00 per month and $2,920 per year. If you are a smoker, I ask you, in the words of Tim McGraw, "How bad do you want it?" This is your dream we are talking about. If you have never had a reason to quit, you have one now. That annual cost could pay for a full year of your community college tuition. If you can't go cold turkey, cut back to half the amount you smoke now and save enough to pay for one semester.

Drinking varies greatly from person to person. There are those who only drink socially. Others will have a couple of glasses of wine one or two nights a week and still others may drink every day. To make my point, I will focus on the once or twice a week drinker of moderately–priced wine. Usually when one opens a bottle of wine, they tend to finish it. An inexpensive bottle can cost about $10. Even at the minimum, the cost of one bottle of wine per week would amount to $520 per year. Keep in mind, that does not include the cost of social drinking, hard liquor, or entertaining. Think about what it costs to order a drink in a restaurant. The cost of that one drink tends to equal the cost of that bottle of wine. A $10 bottle of wine may sell for $25 in a restaurant. If you cut back even a little, you could save enough to buys books for a semester.

I can hear some of you saying that you may need that occasional drink to get through the tough times. We all need to unwind now and then, but if you can just begin to make some adjustments here and there, you will be surprised at how much the little changes will make in your ability to save.

Another area that can become costly is the money spent on buying coffee. For many of us, that daily cup of Starbucks or Dunkin' Donuts or 7- Eleven becomes a ritual that requires no thought after a while, so much so that we forget how much we shell out for that cup of morning Joe. If we take the price of the smallest cup of Starbuck's coffee at $1.65 for just the weekdays, that averages $400 a year. Add to that the days you stop by in the afternoon for a mocha latte at $3.40, and your total is upwards of $600.

You should not have to give up the things you enjoy; however, consider asking about special offers from your favorite coffee stop. For instance, the 7-Eleven franchise offers its customers 99 cent coffee refills if you purchase their travel mug. That is half the price of the standard cup of coffee. These kinds of options can cut your present expense in half, saving you money that could be put toward purchasing books for a semester.

Have you gotten the picture yet? You need to take stock of your life and figure out what things you can do without. There are many products that can be purchased generically without sacrificing quality. Your little ones aren't going to know the difference between that 99 cent box of cookies and a $3.50 package of Oreos. When my children were little, I did just that– purchased the store brand of chocolate sugar cookies. The kids called them "9 mile cookies" because there were about 60 cookies in the package. Yet, they still ate and enjoyed them! The choices are many, and they differ for each of us. Just keep reminding yourself of the importance of your sacrifices.

***

Today there are so many more options for adults to take advantage of. With all of the new technology out there, it is no longer necessary to limit yourself or to believe that you must attend the best four-year college to get ahead. Think about what is best for you. Do the research, and talk to people. You may be overlooking what is right in front of you. Your local community college may have just the right program to get you to your goal, and it will be much more affordable. For some professions, for example, radiology, completing a degree may not be necessary. A vocational program offered through the hospital may be all you need. In other cases, you may just need to take courses to enhance your knowledge in a particular field.

A perfect example is that of Mark Thompson, former executive at Charles Schwab. Mr. Thompson has written many books on the subject of moving ahead and taking risks. In his 40s, he realized his company needed to keep up with growing internet technology so he went back to college to expand his understanding of web design. As he explained in an interview with Julia Savacool from *USA Weekend,* "It was me and a bunch of 20 year olds." Sound familiar? Like many of us, he took courses part time and later became the executive producer of Schwab.com. Mark Thompson practiced what he preached.

Frank Lloyd Wright tells us: "I know the price of success: dedication, hard work, and an unremitting devotion to the things you want to see happen." If you truly have this devotion, not only will these choices be attainable, but you will come up with many more of your own. Remember, the satisfaction of achievement, along with the difference in the salary you will earn, will more than compensate for the money you will spend to get there.

Our ambition should be to rule ourselves, the true kingdom for each of us; and true progress is to know more, and be more, and to do more.

Oscar Wilde

Chapter 13

Knowing What's Best for You

Often adults who come to seek my advice ask, "How can I know what is best for me?" It is an excellent question that is on the minds of many, and the answer is the same for all: you need to begin with self-exploration. It is not always best to do what we are good at. We limit ourselves to only that with which we are already familiar.

Remember, when I first started to think about college, I only knew I was good at working with children. My first assumption was that I would teach preschoolers in nursery school. I had no self-confidence and could never imagine myself earning a bachelor's degree, not to mention a master's degree. Because I had no self-confidence, I set low goals for myself, goals that would not necessarily require advanced schooling. I had done no self-exploration nor did I seek the advice of any professionals. However, as I explained earlier, I had carefully selected my courses in order to buy myself time.

The lack of exploration might have worked against me had it not been for the advice of one of my first professors. I might have wasted time and credits going in a direction that was wrong for me.

It was my psychology professor who recognized my interest in his subject and asked about my career goals. I explained my plans to finish my associate's degree and work in a nursery school. The resulting conversation went something like this:

"Why not go for the full NY state teacher certification?" He asked.

"That would take too long and be so much more work. I just don't think I can accomplish all that," I responded.

"First of all," he continued, "time goes very quickly. Secondly, why do you think you can't accomplish it? You're doing very well in this class, and this is a difficult subject."

"Thank you for the reassurance," I answered, "but I don't know. This is my first time in college, and I'm almost 40. I can't afford to spend a lot of years and a lot of money on school and . . ."

The professor interrupted, "So you're 40; where are you going? Don't you feel that you are worth the time? If it takes you four or five or six years, you'll still be using your time at something. Would you rather look back with regrets?"

I listened in amazement. It was like I was hearing the words I had read from "Dear Abby." The same advice that motivated me to begin this new endeavor was now there to remind me of what I should do. However, I still was not convinced and continued to allow excuses to get in the way, as I answered,

"But what's wrong with teaching in a nursery school?"

"Nothing, if you're happy earning $9.00 an hour," he said.

"But, I can work my way up. Maybe I can eventually become a director or even own a nursery school and earn more money," I replied.

"Listen," he continued, "why don't you go home and make some calls. Call nursery schools and ask them two questions. First, what are the requirements for becoming a nursery school teacher, and second, what is the salary a teacher earns and the salary a director earns."

I was puzzled by his suggestions. "Isn't the early childhood program for those interested in teaching preschool?" I asked.

"Yes," he responded, "and it is an excellent degree but is it a requirement, or can you get the job without it? That's what I want you to find out. Look in one of those local newspapers like *The Penny Saver* where you'll find plenty of ads." He obviously knew the answer but now I was intrigued and couldn't wait to make the phone calls and hear the answers for myself.

My professor was driving me to do the exploration I should have already done. I was impressed by the honesty of the first nursery school director I called who admitted that the average teacher salary remained at $8.00 - $9.00 an hour and a college degree was not needed to own or operate a preschool. I asked about advancement, and she graciously admitted that it depended on what the director could afford, but at best, it was minimal. She explained that most teachers will continue their schooling in order to advance to state level. I called two more schools, and each brought me to the same conclusion: if I wanted to earn a decent salary, I would need to get certified.

Now that I had the information, what would I do with it? How should I proceed? There were so many questions going through my mind. Did I really want to continue for a four-year degree? And how long will that four-year degree actually take as a part-time student? Five years? Six years? And if teaching is what I really want to do, won't I eventually need a master's degree? Maybe I was looking at 10 years of schooling ahead of me. Should I do it? *Could* I do it? Then there was one very important unanswered question: what about the cost? How can I afford to go to school for all the years it would take to complete these degrees?

So many questions clouded my mind, leaving me with feelings of uncertainty and wondering what I had gotten myself into. Still, I wasn't willing to give up. A quote I had read by William Ellery Channing seemed appropriate at that moment: "Difficulties are meant to rouse, not discourage." I didn't know who the wise speaker was, but I knew I should heed his words if I wanted to move forward — and so should you!

That which does not kill us, only makes us stronger

Frederick Nietchze

Chapter 14

Making the Right Preparations

By now, if you are anything like me, you are feeling very overwhelmed at the amount of work it will take to reach your goal. Ask yourself if there has been anything important in your life that has come easy. Has there been anything worth waiting for that didn't take patience and endurance and hard work and dedication? Then why should this venture be different? Those are the thoughts I had when I was overcome with doubt and frustration. It was at times like these that I would remember Dear Abby's advice and take a deep breath and move forward, just as I did when my psychology professor's advice proved true.

That following Saturday after psychology class, I reported my findings on preschool research. Instead of responding with the predictable, "I told you so," My professor asked:

"So now that you have this information, what are you going to do about it?"

I told him I wasn't sure what the next step should be but one thing I was sure of, I wasn't giving up. He graciously offered his reliable advice on the appropriate course of study to take for transferability to the four-year school. His advice was of vital importance to my academic career.

Remember this: if you are going to take on this enormous endeavor, make sure to seek proper advice for the best direction to take. Talk to a professional, be it an academic advisor, a college counselor or one of your professors. Let them know about your personal situation, any issues you may have or obstacles that may interfere with your goals. Most importantly, ask questions!

How many times have you heard that in reference to a doctor's visit? A good doctor will want to know your background and your family history in order to help you make the right choices for your personal well-being. Try to think of this in the same way. These people are trained to help you find the right path. Don't be intimidated, as I was. Making the wrong choices can cost you time and money; both are valuable assets that must not be taken for granted. This is your career; your journey to a new beginning.

Had I initially sought advice, I would have saved myself a lot of stress. Begin thinking about what you want to know about college and plan the questions accordingly. Whether you are unsure about what to study or the qualifications of certain majors or the resources available to fit your needs, take the opportunity to learn all you can from the professionals who are there to help you.

Once you take that first step, I urge you to go one step further. Do your own research as well! Of course, not everyone is fortunate enough to know exactly what they want to be when they grow up — remember I wasn't — but there are steps you can take to get to that point. Keep in mind that everything I tell you I have experienced and have had to do myself.

Consider your situation. How far are you willing to travel from home to school? Do you need to take classes at night? Do you have children's schedules to work around? Do you work full-time or part-time? Do you have previous credits that could transfer? Are you aware of the requirements and the time it will take to complete your degree? These are questions I ask prospective adult students who want to attend college classes. Let's address some of these questions as we would if you were sitting in front of me.

What do you want to be when you grow up?
✱✱✱

Some prospective students come to see me knowing exactly what they want to do. They want to enroll in our nursing program or become a fitness specialist or a teacher. For them, the mission is easier because the requirements are detailed in the school catalog and must be followed step by step. However, sometimes prerequisites are needed before admission into these programs, causing plans to be disrupted for some.

I should explain that a prerequisite is a course needed in advance of another course. For example, before students can sign up for a science course, they must demonstrate proficiency in elementary algebra. Sometimes the knowledge that more time and energy is needed causes students to become stressed and ready to give up. That is when I reassure them and encourage them to take one step at a time. Other students know they want to make something of themselves but are not sure where to begin. That was me. The advantage they have over me is that they are coming to seek out advice before they start the venture. Many are intimidated at first, as I was, but once we engage in conversation, and I reveal my own experiences, the pressure begins to subside, and they are left feeling at ease.

Feeling at ease with your decision is essential because you need to be your own best advocate. When I speak with adults who desire to take the plunge, I know they are committed to their decision but the insecurity is still there. I can easily recognize this, having been there myself. You need to remember that many have successfully accomplished great things later in life, and many will continue to do so. My belief is that if you are motivated, and you believe you can, then you will. Once you are convinced of this, you can begin to figure out what you want to do.

My Advice: Consider a Liberal Arts Degree

***

My best advice for a new college student with no definitive plan is to take liberal arts. This degree is what most four-year colleges and universities will require of new students in the first two years. The advantage of following this degree is twofold. First, it requires the math, science, humanities, and social sciences courses that will be needed later to satisfy the requirements for the bachelor's degree, and, secondly, it allows you to take courses in unfamiliar areas in order to explore your interests. Most liberal studies degrees will include three to four elective courses that are generally unrestricted, allowing students to try subjects in a variety of areas. Another good use of electives is to satisfy courses required in the subsequent four year college.

On the advice of my psychology professor, I enrolled in the liberal arts degree program at the end of my first semester. This allowed me to take a variety of courses to determine what I was good at and what interested me in terms of teaching, while being careful to select courses that would also transfer to the university. It was during this time, at the community college, that I discovered my interest in teaching American history which was an unusual choice for me because I never had an interest in history when I was younger.

How far are you willing to travel?

***

If you are a single person with no obstacles or family dependents, then the location for where you attend school may not be a concern. You may be ready to make a change and therefore choosing a school out of town or out of state may be good for you. However, if you are a family man or woman with or without children, this is an important consideration. Maybe you work full-time and commute up to an hour to and from your job. In this case, you may consider choosing a college near your workplace. Some colleges and universities have multiple campuses that will allow you the flexibility to take some courses near your workplace and some on the weekend near home.

Perhaps you are a stay-at-home parent who needs to wait for someone to relieve you in the evening. The campus location, as well as the time you choose for your evening course, must be considered. Professors hate to have students strolling into class late and interrupting the lecture, so, it is important to allow yourself ample time to get to class. Don't take the attitude that it is okay to arrive late once in a while. Some professors will deduct credit from your grade for lateness.

This holds true for the time it takes to pick up your child from school. Do not assume it will be okay to leave class early to get to the bus on time. These are the issues that should be considered prior to making your schedule. Don't sign up for a class that ends at the same time your children get off the school bus because you assume the teacher will not mind if you leave ten minutes early. On the contrary, professors have little patience for students who begin packing up before they are dismissed. I tell you from experience: as a professor, I make a point of letting students know that they are being rude and should be paying attention to my lesson instead of the clock on the wall.

My Advice: Consider the Community College

***

Some may have negative connotations about community colleges; don't believe them. A community college is close to home, more affordable, and has all of the same requirements to prepare you for moving up to the university or four year college. Most are guided by the requirements of the state and fall under the state university system. For example, Suffolk County Community College, the college I attended, is part of SUNY, the State University of New York. As such, it is governed by the same general education requirements as four-year colleges and universities that are part of SUNY. This allows smooth transferability for students planning to achieve their bachelor's degree at one of the state universities. For years I have been educating students about the benefits of completing their freshman and sophomore years at community college before transferring elsewhere. Let me explain why.

In two years, you can be sitting next to students at the University at Stony Brook, NYU, Harvard or any other school in the nation, who will have started there as freshmen. The only difference is that those students spent a lot more money than you will have spent as a transfer student.

Another benefit to consider is size. Often the community college is smaller than the university or four-year college. This means smaller classes, and as a result, a more intimate learning environment. In a classroom of 30 students, you will be more than just a number, and you are apt to be more comfortable asking questions, as opposed to a lecture hall of 200–plus students where the professor cannot possibly get to know any one of them. This can make a difference in the learning experience. I have always made the effort to build rapport with each of my professors, but once I transferred to the university, it was much more difficult, and often intimidating. I can only imagine how much more difficult this would have been had I started my journey at the larger institution rather than at the community college.

If you have previous credits, will they transfer?
***

Some of you may be returning to college with credits previously accumulated. In that case, it may be beneficial for you to consider the university or four-year college initially. To best make this determination, have your transcripts sent to the institution you are considering. All colleges and universities have a transcript evaluator who can assess your courses and determine whether the credits can be accepted by the institution. This can usually be found on the college website. Once you've taken the initial step, allow a couple of weeks before following through. You should always follow-up correspondence with an in-person appointment where you can have your questions answered. It is important to have a clear understanding of the school's requirements and expectations. This is especially important for adults who are attending classes part-time because most institutions don't provide orientation sessions for those students taking one or two classes. Remember, this is your turn and your opportunity to take control of your future.

Of course, you are not expected to have your entire college career decided on day one; however, it is never too soon to begin thinking about where you will transfer once you have determined your course of study. Then the issue to consider is which school or university has the major you are interested in? This may affect your decision. It did mine.

What is required and how much time will it take to complete your degree?

***

Once I had made the decision to go for a teaching certification, elementary education seemed to make the most sense. However, my research revealed there were no affordable colleges in my area with that degree program. Remember, I had three children and needed to be close to home. Consequently, my school of choice was Stony Brook University where the only teaching programs offered were in secondary education. I wasn't sure how I felt about teaching grades seven through twelve but I had no choice. A private college was not an option as the tuition was three times the cost of the state university. In addition, the location was so convenient; it was just a couple of miles north of where I was living. My decision was made; once I had completed my associate's degree, I would transfer to Stony Brook and enroll in the secondary education teacher certification degree for social studies.

Now I needed to find out what requirements of the four-year school could be satisfied at the community college. There were actually three courses that were required at both institutions: statistics, foreign language and study of another culture. My research revealed that whether math was needed for your degree program or not, statistics is the minimum math proficiency course every student must complete to graduate from Stony Brook. If you are anything like me, and math is not your strong point, you will want to make sure you satisfy this requirement at the community college level. Even after I had passed the course and satisfied the graduation requirement, I had to take a math proficiency test when I transferred. The results of that test would have placed me in a lower level of math had I not already taken and passed statistics.

The next requirement took a lot more work in every sense of the word. I learned that Stony Brook's foreign language requirement could be waived with an earned grade of at least 75 on the high school Regents, so I set out to search back 25 years for my grade on the Spanish Regents. After filling out many forms and making numerous phone calls, the bad news arrived in the mail. My grade was a 74! It might as well have been a failing grade. It was bad enough I had to take math; now I had to figure out how to get through Spanish. I remember thinking, "I'm too old for this stuff!"

Now I know, and I remind you, not to look at your life as growing older, but only as growing! I truly believe that age is just a number and some days we feel 80 and some days we feel 25 again.

In the end, my decisions to take these courses at the community college paid off. I successfully completed them, and while they were not my best grades, they all transferred easily into my degree requirements at the university, leaving me free to concentrate on my major. Conversely, many of my Stony Brook classmates transferred without the required courses and after enrolling in foreign language and statistics, they dropped out opting to take those classes at the community college during the summer.

The choices you make early in your academic career can have a positive or negative impact later, so it is important to know the ramifications of your decisions and choose wisely. As twentieth century French philosopher, Albert Camus said, "Life is the sum of all your choices."

The only good is knowledge and the only evil is ignorance

Socrates

Chapter 15

Making Technology Work for You

When I was attending the community college, technology was not as broad as it is today. All of my courses were taught in the classroom, aside from a couple of telecourses. These fully accredited college courses included televised programs that could be recorded and watched at one's convenience, with independent assignments distributed at the first class meeting. They were extremely convenient for me as I continued to juggle my family responsibilities along with my academic obligations.

When it comes to distance education, online courses have now largely replaced the telecourse. In fact, some colleges offer full degrees through this method. While I have never taken an online course, I know many students who have successfully completed degree requirements in this manner.

When my daughter was completing her master's degree, she enjoyed taking many of her required English courses online. I couldn't understand how this process worked well in the field of literature, but Jenn pointed out that there was more interaction among the students through this online method than she had often experienced in the classroom. She explained that many students are intimidated speaking out in the classroom, but behind a computer screen, they are more comfortable and more apt to contribute to the discussion and even ask questions. Also with this type of course, students have the freedom to work at their leisure. So if you work all day, and you're a night owl, you might find it convenient and preferable to check in with your classmates at midnight. A stay-at-home parent might prefer attending class before the household awakens at five in the morning. Remember, these sessions, regardless of your choice of time, are in place of physically attending class on campus. The professor will usually require a certain amount of online involvement but the actual time preference is up to you, which is why this method is so convenient to many adults with full schedules and limited availability in the conventional school day.

***

The benefit of online courses extends far beyond your average day. Remember, this is the internet! You can attend class everywhere and anywhere you are at any moment. Are you planning a family vacation to Disney World? No worries, you can take that trip, and you don't have to miss class.

When I was attending Stony Brook, we had a trip planned in March. I couldn't afford to miss class or fall back on assignments so we worked our vacation around my class schedule. Class was held on Tuesday night, so we went to the resort from Wednesday to Monday. Each day I would retreat to the beach with my textbook and notepad to find a nice shade hut where I could read the works of Oscar Wilde and other masters of English literature. Of course, it was a pleasure to be surrounded by sand and shore on a lounge chair while reading poetry and prose, but today even that can be improved upon with the flexibility an online class offers.

Another option that is popular in many multi-campus colleges is "synchronous distance education." This differs from online courses in that students may take a course that is offered at one campus while sitting in a facility at another campus. The courses are taught via satellite, and the participants can interact with each other through a screen on which all the classrooms are projected. The instructor remains at the home campus and can see all of the students, and all of the students can see the instructor.

This type of course is convenient for the student who cannot travel from one campus to another but wishes to take a particular course offered at another facility. Some of you may be familiar with this concept as it is frequently used for meetings in the business world.

More specific types of programs, tailored to your needs, may be available at the college you choose. It's important for you to make inquiries and do your research. You will often find this information easily on the college website, particularly if it is a new program the college is trying to promote.

Maya Angelou tells us: "Do the best you can until you know better. Then when you know better, do better."

Our doubts are traitors, and make us lose the good we oft might win by fearing to attempt.

Shakespeare

Chapter 16

Believing you Can

The preparations that you make at the start of your journey will continue throughout your years at college. Every schedule you make, every course you take, every semester you complete will affect your academic outcome. Yes, you can find motivation in the words I write here, and yes, it will help to lean on your supporters along the way. However, the greatest preparation you will need — the training, the homework, the studying, and of course, the papers, that will be required of you each and every week of each and every semester— is your own.

As difficult as it is to get started, the journey itself can become overwhelming at times. It is those times when your commitment will be seriously challenged, and your determination to succeed will need to be strengthened. Nothing I say here on these pages is meant to diminish the amount of effort that will be needed on your part. I won't pretend that motivation and determination is enough to get you through. It's hard! And there will be plenty of times when you will question why you wanted to put yourself through this. I did, many times! In fact, there were times when it was easier to agree with the cynics than to believe in myself.

So what's the point of all this? The point is exactly this: I did it, and you can do it too. Allow yourself to feel those feelings, and then move on. I felt frustrated, I cried, I got angry and sad. Other times I felt happiness and elation and pride. Sometimes I could experience all of these emotions in the same week. If you are wondering how that could be or if I'm exaggerating, it was, and I'm not. I still have vivid images in my mind of myself sitting at my kitchen counter, head in hands, books open in front of me, tears rolling down my face, thinking, "When does this get easier?" Other times I'd think, "I want my old life back!"

On those occasions, it was difficult for me to absorb anything. No matter how many times I'd read the lines on the pages in front of me, they were just empty words that would not sink in. It was like having writer's block and staring at an empty page. I soon learned to stop fighting it and accept that those were times when I would need to take a step back and give myself a break.

You can't move forward if you allow the frustrations to take over. Believe that it's ok to have those feelings, and pick up the phone to talk to someone who will boost your morale, or go out for a walk or a bike ride. If you can't exercise the mind, use that time to exercise the body. The fresh air will clear your head and help you find the stamina to continue.

You should not underestimate the importance of your strength of mind. If the process of attaining your goal is to be successful, it can only be accomplished with your own determination and your continued belief in your dream. Think about all of the issues that are clogging your brain. Are you a parent with small children tugging at you for attention? Maybe you have children of school age who need your help with homework after school while you're getting dinner ready and preparing your own work for class. Maybe you work and have to rush off to school immediately afterwards. Or worse, maybe all of the above applies to you, as it did to me. This may help you understand why, at times, my frustration level led me to cry often and feel as though I was having a breakdown.

Back when I first started my college career, each day began with getting my own two of three children off to school. Within minutes, I'd again have three children to care for and more breakfast and lunch to prepare along with the cleaning and laundry and playtime. The schoolwork was usually accomplished sitting on my front steps while the three little ones played.

After three o'clock, the three became five, and there was homework to supervise and sometimes ballet lessons to drive to or the library or after school sports or activities to get to or from. Dinner would be ready for five o'clock, right after the girls were picked up so that on class nights, I could be out of the house by 5:30.

Once inside the classroom, it became necessary to shut out the world and transfer my concentration to academics, a requirement that was not always easy. For three hours, I was not mommy or chauffeur or homemaker; I was student. The problem was it didn't end in the classroom. The amount of homework required in between classes was difficult to manage. Life just got in the way, and at times, I didn't know how or where to find a gap.

From there it got harder, and my life got more congested. After my first year at the community college, my youngest son was ready to start school so I was ready to attend college full time. My friend's children were also starting school, making my decision easier. Soon I learned I could get part-time work at the college so one job got replaced with another. It wasn't much, but being a college aide would allow me the flexibility to work around my course schedule as well as my children's schedule. I could see them off at the bus in the morning, go to class, go to work, then go home in time to get them off the bus, assist with the homework, do all the after school driving and prepare dinner. Since it was only a 17– hour work week, I still had two free days to devote to studies and papers. In those two days, I would also take care of cleaning the house, laundry and food shopping. It worked; it wasn't easy, but it worked for me.

***

My connection to the college, as both a student and a worker, was an important step in the right direction for my future goals, so, I had to do it all, and do it to the best of my ability. That is why, at times, the frustration level was more than I could handle, and I was doing nothing to lighten my load. At the time, it just did not seem feasible. I didn't want to give up the job as it was my small contribution to the household, and it was my connection to the education field. I certainly was not willing to give up going to school as that was my path to a future career in education; of course giving up my first job as wife, mother and homemaker wasn't an option.

So, instead, as I moved ahead in my education, I continued to add responsibilities without taking any away. My drive sometimes exceeded my common sense. I was tired but I couldn't stop. I was drained and frustrated but I couldn't give in. I'd waited too long to get started and couldn't waste any more time. Even now, I'm sometimes exhausted from working all day at my 9 – 5 job, only to go home and put in hours at the computer. However, I have to keep at it, in part for the same reasons that I had when I was attending college while juggling all of my family responsibilities: I want others to believe that, regardless of age, it is never too late to get started on your dream.

As C. S. Lewis told us, "You are never too old to set another goal or to dream a new dream."

If you believe it will work out, you'll see opportunity. If you believe it won't, you'll see obstacles.

Dr. Wayne Dyer

Chapter 17

Still Believing

While everything I've been describing can be viewed as obstacles, once you've reached the point referred to earlier by Kafka, "the point where you will no longer turn back," you must see only opportunity. I would have never gotten through my associate's, my bachelor's and my two master's degrees if I saw only obstacles and let them stand in my way.

Thinking back on various occurrences, I sometimes wonder how I made it through. My mission continued to get more difficult when I transferred to Stony Brook University. I'd begun to feel secure at the community college, and now the fears surfaced again. I had heard how large the university was and how the classrooms were lecture halls—some as big as movie theaters. It would be like starting all over again, not knowing anyone, feeling lost and out of place. But, once again, what choice did I have? So many times Kafka's words are what got me to the next step, through the next hurdle. They helped me believe that I had no choice but to move forward, like the day I was expected to report for orientation to my new college.

The postcard read, "Plan to be there from 8:30 to 4:00." I wondered what could possibly be expected of me for almost eight hours. My answer included a placement test, lectures, speaking with instructors, building my schedule and visiting the nurse. That last one baffled me since I was over the age of needing to prove MMR, (vaccination for measles, mumps and rubella); still, I went through all of the motions, as was expected of me. On that busy day, there was one moment that stood out and clearly resonates with me even today.

Early in the day, about a hundred of us were ushered into a lecture hall and told to take a seat. Just as I wondered if that was what my classes would be like, a loud bang, followed by a deep, firm voice came from the front of the hall. The tall-young man introduced himself as an advisor who was there to assist us with our passage into the next level. But the turning point came when he held up the university's bulletin, the book he had just slammed on the lectern, and said to the group:

"See this book? This has to be your bible from now until the day you graduate. Read it, and memorize every page because you are responsible for knowing the requirements of this university." He continued lecturing us in a serious tone and ended with this final, intimidating statement:

"Don't come to us two weeks before graduation and say no one told you that you needed this or that, because, if it's in this book, it's your responsibility to know it and to follow the requirements."

Most of us sat there silently taking in his words. He told us in no uncertain terms what was expected of us and if we messed up, we would have no one to blame but ourselves. I've never forgotten those words and until this day, I relate that story to my students so that they can begin preparing themselves to be independent, inquiring adults from day one.

My days at Stony Brook were rewarding but increasingly difficult. As an undergraduate, most of my classes were in the huge lecture halls that I'd been warned about. Some held as many as 500 students; most averaged 250. I made a point of sitting front and center in every class to get to know the professor. I soon realized that, even in the orchestra seats, there was no getting to know a professor in that atmosphere. The classes were so large that some did not even bother to take attendance. What was most surprising was the number of students who took advantage of this by only showing up on the first day, the day of midterms and the day of the final exam. I wondered how they could be successful in the course. I could not imagine grasping the material on my own. The amount of notes I took filled binders, yet, in class after class, there were these students who were satisfied just getting by.

In some ways, I envied them. I envied their freedom to do nothing but take classes. Many of them had the luxury of living on campus. They didn't need to work; their only responsibility was to attend school. I wondered if they knew how lucky they were. But it didn't matter; I knew I couldn't skip class even if I wanted to. I needed that interaction and the hundreds of notes I wrote from every lecture. The classroom was my place of learning, and outside the classroom was where reinforcement took place.

I was majoring in secondary education with an emphasis in American history for teaching social studies. Soon after the required coursework was completed, I was expected to enroll in student teaching in a high school. That's when I really started to feel like I was losing it. My schedule was so overloaded, and the workload so heavy, that, at times, I could not remember where I was supposed to be at any given moment.

I still recall the poster hanging in one of the offices at the college, on which was written: "Winners are committed to 'hang in' there long enough to win." The author cleverly posted his words beneath a picture of a healthy little tree holding its own on the edge of a mountainside.

Christine Crowe

Whenever things get tough, just remember, every flower that ever bloomed had to go through a whole lot of dirt to get there!

Anonymous

Chapter 18

Lecture halls and holidays and migraines, oh my!

Student teaching was my opportunity to prove how good a teacher I would be. I shopped for dresses and suits that would make a professional appearance. I wanted everything to be perfect; I wanted to get a job as a teacher, and I believed I could.

My cooperating teacher was very thorough and made sure I took part in every aspect of the teaching day. This included morning and afternoon department meetings, faculty lunches and after school activities. I was expected to make my own lesson plans, tests, quizzes, and grade all assignments. While experiencing the full spectrum of teaching, I was also made aware of what it was like to have another full-time job on top of my part-time job, my family responsibilities, and my night classes.

A typical day for me included working at the high school from 7:30 in the morning until 2:30 in the afternoon. From there, I traveled about 14 miles to my job at the community college and worked from 3:00 until 7:00, three nights a week, 3:00 until 6:00 on Thursdays and 2:30 until 5:00 on Fridays. On Thursdays, I went from student teaching to my part-time job, to the university to take my last two required courses, getting home on those nights at 10:00 o'clock. This continued for a full semester.

There were days I would get into my car and forget which direction to drive. Was this a school day? Was it a work day? I truly didn't know whether I was coming or going. One afternoon I drove the 14 miles to my part-time job at the community college, only to realize I was not expected to work that day and I could have just gone home after my student teaching. Home was right down the block from where I was teaching.

Keep in mind, I was still doing my own homework and writing papers, studying, reading and preparing for midterms and finals. This was in conjunction with my other full-time job as mom and homemaker. I would often sense the disappointment of my three children who would be looking forward to family time at 8:00 p.m. when I'd return home exhausted. Sometimes on the weekends, the work would get so overwhelming that I had to stay home buried in my books while my husband took the kids out to a movie. My concentration needed to be on my work but my heart wished to be out with my family.

***

At certain times of the year, the stress was more intense. This was particularly true in the fall semesters with the excitement and hustle and bustle of the holidays. For most of my life, the days between Thanksgiving and Christmas were filled with anticipation, and joy, and family activity. This all changed in the years I was a student. Instead of reveling in the joy of the holiday season, I was overwhelmed by it. Studying, papers and preparing for finals was added to the tasks of shopping and wrapping gifts. On top of that, were parties I was expected to attend through the high school, luncheons at my part-time job, and gifts to buy for co-workers and my cooperating teacher.

It was during those busy months that I started to get migraine headaches. At times, the headaches were so bad that I would get violently sick to my stomach. Each episode was like a dreaded, unwelcome visitor. The pressure in my head, the nausea, and the constant throbbing that emanated from the back of my neck led to vomiting. It would come from out of nowhere with no warning. It happened at school and at work; it even hit me while driving.

Yes, a migraine came over me while driving on the Long Island Expressway. Returning home from Stony Brook at 65 miles an hour in the left lane, I started to feel the pressure engulf me, followed by the nausea. Within minutes, I knew I was going to be sick, and there was nowhere to escape. I remember thinking, *this can't be happening; I have to make it home.* My anxiety only exacerbated the pain but I could not stop. On the passenger seat was my hat, that only minutes before, had shielded me from the rain. Without a second thought, I reached over and grabbed what would become my barf bag for the rest of my drive, and somehow I made it home safely.

Another time, also while driving on the expressway; all I had in my reach was the scarf around my neck. Fortunately, it was large enough to keep me from ruining my clothes or my car. However, I ruined a brand new cashmere scarf that would never be worn again.

The headaches continued throughout my semesters at Stony Brook. There was a morning, on my way to work at the community college that I began to feel the sensation of nausea. This time I was able to pull over to the side of the road to get sick, allowing me to avoid ruining more articles of clothing. Afterwards, as I sat still for a moment with my eyes closed, a man approached my car to ask if I was alright. I responded that I would be, thanked him and continued my drive to work. Later that morning, our office receptionist introduced me to her husband who had come by to drop something off and to my embarrassment; it was the same gentleman who offered me help that morning.

Episodes like these, brought on by stress, were becoming commonplace for me, so it became necessary to carry prescription medication that could be taken at the first sensation of an impending headache. But the stress still showed up in other ways. There was the time when my car ran out of gas on the way to school. Rushing off to class, in traffic, after dinner with the family, my mind was on the assignments due that night. *Were they written correctly? Did I study enough? What if I'm asked to discuss the readings?* With all this on my mind, I never thought to look down at the gas gauge. Halfway to school, my car stalled, and only then did I realize I was out of gas. Fortunately, I w less than a block from a gas station where I could get helr I didn't realize was that there was a $20.00 fee to fill · and bring it out of the station, in addition to the ℯ

I won't try to convince you that str while undertaking a new venture. I won' magic stress busters. What I will sugges' best of you, consider looking up the Yourself Up," and try to follow the ′ King Cole.

Don't let one cloud obliterate the whole sky.

Anais Nin

Chapter 19

"C" is a Respectable Grade

Yes, that is what I meant to say. Those words were said to me by a dean of students early in my academic learning. I did not understand why he would say that, nor did I agree with him back then, but I do now. I was so serious about my studies; I would accept nothing less than perfection, no matter how difficult that was to achieve. Unfortunately, at times, it was too difficult for me and, as a result, so was acceptance. Now I recognize this as a common behavior for many of my adult students.

The first time I received a less than stellar grade was in an introductory computer class. I expected it to be a hands-on course that would teach me to use basic programs needed for writing papers and emails. Instead, it was a very technical course requiring a lot of reading and studying about the history of the computer dating back to the days when IBM was the only name in town. I worked hard at keeping up. I read and I tried to memorize page after page of technological material but I could not get it to sink in. My instructor was aware of the difficulty I was experiencing and how hard I was trying, so she offered to help me with extra tutoring. Unfortunately, it didn't sufficiently help my understanding, so, I considered withdrawing at the mid-semester point. My instructor convinced me to stick it out and told me she would sign a withdrawal form if I still wanted to drop the course before the end of the semester. I took her advice but still felt disappointment when my grade for the course was a C+.

At the time, I was working as a college aide for the dean of students. And it was after this happened that the dean made that statement to me about how a C is a respectable grade. I know it was his way of reassuring me that it was okay to get less than an A in a course, but I still felt somewhat beaten down. All of the doubts and questions came rushing back. Fortunately, I was the only one who did not believe in me; my supporters were much kinder in their responses than I was to myself.

The second time I received a disappointing grade was even more devastating than the first. It was in my senior year of college at the university. The course was Adolescent Psychology, a subject I thoroughly enjoyed. I had no difficulty keeping up with the assignments, but the grading was based solely on a midterm and a final, which were both multiple choice tests, so the answers were either right or wrong. There was no discretion as would be the case with written essays, and for me, this proved to be disastrous. I am a writer; therefore, I am more comfortable with expressing and explaining my thinking through written responses. As a result, I did poorly on both tests and in the end, all of my hard work in the course counted for nothing. I was graded solely on the results of the midterm and the final, which, I am embarrassed to say, resulted in a grade of D+.

This was incomprehensible to me. I had never sunk that low before that course or in any subsequent course. I felt the need to speak to my professor, but to no avail. What was interesting, however, was her surprise when she realized that I was the person who matched the name and the grade. This was one of those lecture halls of 250 students where the instructor rarely gets to know anyone personally. Because I sat front and center, my face was recognizable as the serious student who took notes and asked questions, so, when I revealed my dismay over the poor grade, the professor felt for me but was unable to change her grading policy. However, she assured me that the course was only one of many psychology courses I would take, and it would not affect my success or need to be retaken.

This took a lot out of me. I knew I should not give up but it took a lot of time and strength and encouragement to believe in myself again. At home, my husband immediately sensed my depressed mood, and when he asked about it, I burst into tears.

Dave was much kinder to me than I was to myself when he said, "It's only one grade; don't let that define you after all the hard work you put into your courses."

Deep down, I knew he was right but I couldn't shake the feeling that I was a failure. How could I expect to teach adolescents if I couldn't master the course? But in time, I had to let go of the doom and gloom and get back to thinking positive. I was too close to success to give up, and fortunately, neither of these courses, in which I had scored poorly, was a prerequisite for entry into my program. Had that been the case, I would have taken the advice I often give to my own students; I would have retaken one or both of these courses.

This is a very important point that you should be fully aware of in your own choice of study. In some cases, even a grade below a B may affect your acceptance into a program or your ability to graduate. The best example I can offer is that of a restricted, competitive program like nursing. At most colleges, restricted programs carry a host of prerequisite courses that must be passed with minimum grades. If these grades are not met, a student's application will not be considered.

***

Think back to my discussion in Chapter 12, and make the right preparations. Seek out the guidance of advisors and professors. Learn the requirements of your chosen area of study and the consequences for not meeting those requirements. Keep in mind that it is not the end of the world if you fail or do poorly. It is at times like these that you also need to draw on your support system. Whether it is listening to words of encouragement from a loved one or recalling an inspirational quote or a reading, you need to hold on to something or someone that can keep you moving forward.

The point of all this is to prepare you for the challenges that may come up along the way. News reporter Ann Curry, in an interview for "USA Weekend," passed on some good advice to working moms that can apply to men and women alike. After explaining the pressures she placed on herself as a young mother, she advises: ". . . forgive yourself for not meeting a standard that really is insane. You're asking too much of yourself." Maybe you don't agree that the standards are insane but we can all agree that we do sometimes ask too much of ourselves. As a result, we should learn to forgive ourselves and continue to move forward even when we fail to meet our expectations.

Confucius offered helpful words of wisdom for just these situations when he said, "Our greatest glory is not in never falling, but in rising every time we fall."

The man who never alters his opinion is like standing water, and breeds reptiles of the mind.

William Blake

Chapter 20

Change is Good

As soon as you begin to get comfortable with the learning and feel like you have an understanding of new concepts and ideas, you will begin to formulate ideas of your own. You will become aware of changes in you and so will your friends and relatives. Some may even oppose the fact that you have changed. Just keep reminding yourself that change is good! Say it out loud if it helps. "Change is good!" Isn't that why you started this venture? As long as you are changing for the better, it is a good thing.

The process of learning will, at the very least, induce both intellectual and emotional changes in you. Don't fight it; don't be intimidated by people's negative reactions to it. Remember, this entire journey is about believing in you. If you are not experiencing growth as you learn, then you are wasting a lot of time, as well as a lot of money.

It was early in my second semester of college when I first started to awaken to self-change. My first English composition class helped me fully recognize my love of writing. But it was in my second semester, in a course titled "Sexism and the Humanities," that I started to experience open-mindedness. The instructor was very aggressive in her approach. She was a true believer in women's liberation and thought that elements of misogyny could be found in everyday life. For example, she would demonstrate hidden messages against women in every commercial and print ad. Given my conservative upbringing, it was difficult for me to accept this "all or nothing" thinking. However, I was able to redeem the value of the course and support the fact that women needed to be independent thinkers and needed to be treated as equals to men. Remember, I was raised in the fifties and sixties. You need only to watch an episode of "Mad Men" to realize that equality between men and women was not the pervasive belief back in that era.

It was also an easily accepted belief by most women, including me. As I said earlier, all I wanted to be when I grew up was a mom like my own mother. I wanted to get married, have children, take care of the household and live happily ever after. That was my only goal, and it was a good one. I didn't go to college because I was unhappy with my situation or to get out of the house; my college career was a precursor to a second career that followed, not replaced, what I did as a homemaker.

As a homemaker, my life was sheltered, and my mind was closed. So when I began to verbalize some of what I was learning in college, I was perceived as a different person; I had changed, and to some, not for the better. I had to learn what I could share and what to keep to myself. Learning helped me become more tolerant and non-judgmental; it piqued my curiosity and encouraged inquiry and examination. For me, there was no superiority complex as I was always conscious of the feelings of others.

That is an important consideration to bear in mind. It can be easy to want to share your knowledge or talk continuously about learning this and learning that but sometimes you may be wise to resist the impulse. Not everyone is interested in hearing the day-to-day progress of your new venture. Think of it like sharing vacation pictures. You captured every wonderful moment of your holiday in photographs, and you look forward to uploading them and reliving the experience. However, others may not be as enthusiastic to participate. When friends and relatives ask us to view their photos, the first few are interesting, but after that, it can get boring. Yet, if the pictures are of your grandchildren, you may enjoy viewing every little detail of every photo. Similarly, there will be those who will ask how your new venture is going and will enjoy hearing about your experiences. Save the sharing for those moments.

This is particularly necessary if you are inclined to correct others. With all your new-found knowledge, your senses may be enhanced in a lot of areas. For me, it has always been English grammar. To this day, I cringe when I hear certain phrases spoken incorrectly. However, I've learned that it is not always wise to bring it up to people. Sometimes, it is ingrained in a person's manner of speaking, and pointing it out will only cause hurt feelings or make me sound like a know-it-all. Since that has never been my intention, I now choose to overlook grammatical errors unless they are spoken or written by my students.

I've learned from Winston Churchill who said, "There is nothing wrong with change, if it is in the right direction."

When one door closes, another door opens but we so often look
so long and so regretfully upon the closed door, that we do not
see the one which has opened for us.

Alexander Graham Bell

Chapter 21

Letting Go of Regrets

Spiritual author Eckhart Tolle devotes an entire book to focusing on the present. He calls it - *The Power of Now.* Tolle explains the negative impacts of dwelling on the past. He says, "The more attention you give to the past, the more you energize it —" He asks his readers: "Does the past take up a great deal of your attention? Are your thought processes creating guilt, pride, resentment, anger, regret or self-pity?" The truth of Eckhart Tolle's message is that staying focused on the past, whether positive or negative, takes away from our focus of what is now.

My son has another way of understanding this concept. David is a successful CPA who has experienced a lot of life, both professionally and personally. In a discussion with him about Tolle's belief for letting go of the past, David offered an economic comparison known as "sunk costs." His simple explanation was that "it's in the past, and it doesn't matter anymore; in other words, it's something that can't be undone or money spent that can't be reversed."

Now with a better understanding of this thinking, I am able to let go of my regrets. I can turn them into productivity and appreciate my present situation or change it. That is not to say that I still don't have negative feelings at times but when these thoughts surface, they are short lived, and I quickly remind myself that stressing over a situation that I cannot change is fruitless. Instead, I can use that energy to change myself and work harder to enjoy my present endeavors, like this writing, for instance.

It is important to learn to let go of regrets or you will never be able to focus on what can be or what is right now. There will always be things in our lives that we wish were different. I wished I had been able to go to college when I was younger, but that was not the case, so what were my options? I could either be satisfied with life as it was or I could overcome the obstacles and find my own way to where I wished to be. Yet even now, after all these years of striving and enjoying success, regret sometimes sneaks into my mind causing me to be distracted from the goodness I have.

The regret that sometimes interferes with my focus is that I did not decide to start college when I was a stay-at-home mom. Looking back, I now recognize all of the ways I could have fit schooling into my schedule while the children were young. Now that I have an excellent job, I realize that if I had started sooner, I could be retired by now and be able to devote more time to writing. At this stage of my life, when many around me are retiring, and I still have a few more years to work, I often feel envy and even self-pity for not being able to retire sooner. But that's not going to happen, so why spend time thinking about things I cannot change? What I've come to realize is that the time spent on what might have been is time taken away from what is now.

The next time that you feel regret, guilt, resentment or even pride for something in your past, take notice. See if you are feeling stressed over it or spending too much time thinking about it. Is it getting in the way of what you should be doing now? Is it counterproductive? What are you going to do about it? Let it go; let go of what you cannot change, and work on what you can.

As Forrest Gump, in the movie of the same name, said, "My Mamma always said you've got to put the past behind you before you can move on."

Anyone who stops learning is old, whether at 20 or 80. Anyone who keeps learning stays young. The greatest thing in life is to keep your mind young.

Henry Ford

Chapter 22

So Many Young Ones

I can fill a book with stories about men and women who have succeeded at learning new things or starting new careers as adults. There were many I've met along my journey and many I've known personally. Not one of these people would tell you it was easy, but all would tell you they were successful in their quest. I believe it productive to highlight some of these success stories for my readers to see the varying degrees of difficulty adults go through on their road to success.

All of the adults I have included here had to make difficult choices at various points in their lives. Each had the option to accept the status quo, which, in most cases, was the easier choice. Instead, they took the more difficult path believing that the end result would provide improvement in their lives.

There is no better quote that sums this up than the following words of Dr. Mehmet Oz as he was being interviewed by WPBF: "My favorite quote from Winston Churchill is, "When you're going through hell, that's no time to turn around. Just keep going."

Liz
✳✳✳

In my role as college professor, teaching in the evening, my classes are often filled with adults striving to reach a new goal. Elizabeth Scala was one of those adult learners taking English 101 in the fall of 2009. As the students took turns introducing themselves, I remember Liz telling us that she was married, had two children, one in elementary school and one in kindergarten, and her goal was to become a registered nurse. She added that she had wanted to go into nursing for a long time, but life got in the way. Now she would do everything it took to reach her goal.

For the next 15 weeks, I watched as Liz dragged herself into class each week, never missing an assignment, copying every note I lectured or wrote on the board. Unlike so many other students, she asked the questions that helped clarify what she didn't understand. In December, her hard work paid off. What started off as a seemingly impossible task ended in a grade of B+. This success brought Liz one step closer to her goal.

Liz would stop by my office occasionally to report on her progress, but the day she came glowing and smiling with excitement, I knew she had gotten accepted into the nursing program. We both knew the amount of work that got her to that point; still, Liz always credited the knowledge she acquired from that English 101 class for arming her with the tools to get there. I knew then that Liz would be a success story that I wanted to write about. Even without yet knowing her story, I saw myself in her. I knew her path would be much more arduous than mine was, simply based on the degree program Liz had chosen to study.

In May 2012, more than five years after Liz left my class, I would learn just how arduous her journey really was. Liz had graduated with her associate's degree in nursing! To fully comprehend her experience, I had to be taken back to the start of her mission. What she told me was eye opening.

Liz was 33 when she had her last child in September of 2003. What started as a joyous time in her life soon became overshadowed by the dark reality of the news she learned a few months later; in spring of 2004, Liz was diagnosed with Hodgkin's lymphoma. It was during that time of constant medical attention, paired with much demonstrative healing and her inability to accomplish even the smallest of everyday tasks that

Liz made up her mind to fulfill her longtime dream of becoming a nurse. But this goal would remain a dream as she watched other nurses care for her, helping her regain her strength after the chemo treatments. With her physical strength building, so also her mental determination was getting stronger. As Liz put it:

"As a survivor, I had to give back. So nursing was going to be my job."

"Why then?" I asked.

"Earlier, I was just not in the mindset for college." She replied.

I asked Liz to take me back to what "earlier" meant for her. Her explanation began not unlike so many others I had heard before.

"In high school, I was not a serious student. The thought of becoming a nurse sounded awesome until I heard of the requisite clinicals. That was just too much work for me to fathom."

As Liz continued to reminisce, I could see her facial expressions change with each recollection.

"I just didn't have the drive back then," Liz confessed somberly. "So when my family moved in my junior year, I enrolled in BOCES for hairdressing and left nursing behind."

Years later, when her younger sister enrolled in NYU, Liz began having regrets. Now thirty years old, just out of a bad relationship, working long hours on her feet in a salon, the thoughts of going to school would surface frequently. While her career was lucrative, it was beginning to wear on her. Even in a happy marriage, Liz felt her life was missing something, but their financial obligations would not allow her to move beyond the thoughts.

After her first child was born, Liz worked part-time as a hairstylist and full-time as a new mom and homemaker. Money was still tight and her dreams seemed to get further pushed aside. It would be years later that Liz began heeding her sister's advice to take that first step and look into the possibility of financial aid for students.

Even then, Liz was concerned with the needs of her family, so she filled out the necessary paper work without her husband's knowledge. It all seemed easy enough, but what she was not prepared for was the college placement exam. She explained,

"It was a disaster! I'd never written any papers in high school so it all seemed so foreign to, and I did terribly in all three areas of the exam. As a result, I became disillusioned and went home crying. It was then that my husband began pushing me and encouraged me to stick with it."

As Liz recalled this time in her life, I could see her face brighten and the pride begin to surface as she informed me of her retest in English that resulted in a better score. I asked Liz to recall the details of her first night in the classroom. Her reply reminded me so much of my own experience on that first night of class.

"I felt old. I was 37, and there I sat staring at a teacher who looked years younger than me. I sat front and center where I was certain not to miss a word. That was math class. I hated that course but knew it was necessary if I wanted to get into nursing. Then I took your class."

"Here it comes," I thought to myself, but Liz continued before I could ask for an explanation.

"From the moment you handed out the syllabus, I knew this was going to be a tough one for me. I hadn't written much in high school and nothing at all since then. But I needed to do well in this class if I was to get accepted into the nursing program. I remember worrying about when I would make the time to fit in all this work."

She explained that a typical day started around 6:00 a.m. making sure the kids were ready for school. She would drop one off at the bus stop and the other at nursery school. It was during those four hours, before the kids needed to be picked up, before the routines would begin again, that she had to fit in the reading, writing and revising required for homework each day. On the weekends, Liz worked at the salon where her boss was not at all supportive, making it difficult to take time off when the workload got heavy.

"On those weekends when a major paper was due, I had no choice but to take off. My husband would take the kids to Connecticut to visit his parents so I could have quiet time to write and do the necessary research. I hated giving up family time, but what choice did I have?"

As Liz continued to relive her experience, I could sense the melancholy in her voice that reminded me of my own angst when I needed to stay home and study or write as my husband took our children to a movie. Like me, family time was very important to Liz, but to achieve the goal, sacrifice was necessary.

Liz continued, "I soon realized that this was only the beginning of the hard work and sacrifices I would have to make. Your class prepared me for what was ahead. As you know, I was accepted into the program, and then, it was like I had no life outside of school work."

Liz explained that acceptance into the program required that she take day classes. That opened up a whole new set of difficulties and life changes for her and her family. Who would get her children off the bus? Who would look after them? There was no one she was close to nearby, and she could not afford child care. She did the only thing she could think of — she put her pride aside and asked her mother for financial help. With that problem solved, she could now focus on her new full-time job.

The increase in her workload, from 3 credits to 14 credits in a semester added to the responsibilities that awaited her at the end of the day. Liz described some of the required courses and tests as "designed to make or break you." It was evident in the details that followed that she narrowly escaped the breaking point!

In the summer of her second year in the program, Liz began experiencing "terrible anxiety."

"I was feeling dizzy all of the time; I feared driving the 10 minute ride to school. Sometimes I felt I was experiencing amnesia as I was becoming forgetful and began having difficulty making decisions. My husband would come home from work to no dinner. We ate a lot of pasta during those times. I tried making lists and having the kids participate in a menu system, which seemed to help." Still, the stress of school did not let up.

Liz turned to her professor hoping for an answer as to why this was happening to her. What she got was a reassurance that it would be ok and a suggestion to listen to relaxation tapes. Of course, this was a good suggestion, but one that seemed too simple for what she was going through, as she continued:

"I was now working with critical patients, and I feared making a mistake and killing them. Some of the procedures I witnessed only made my condition worse. I would stand near walls to avoid falling, often sweating profusely in a state of panic. The results of an MRI and CAT scan showed no cause for my symptoms."

Keep in mind; a typical week for Liz included working full days from Monday through Thursday and continuing to work part time on Saturdays and in the summer. The holidays were a burden rather than a joy — another detail that we had in common. Liz and her husband had to remortgage their house to keep up with expenses. Their family life was deteriorating with Liz snapping at everyone and fighting with her husband.

She literally had no time to take care of herself and, as a result, she developed high blood pressure as the stress continued. She recalled, "The demands of nursing school were so intense and so time consuming, I had no time to focus on life. I remember having to miss my son's regionals in bowling, an event that took place upstate and was to be a family vacation. I almost lost my best friend, who I only called when I needed something."

Fortunately, she added, "The end justified the means!" At the time of this writing, she has passed her boards and is interviewing for jobs. It took her six years of working all year around to get here. Her stress and anxiety have diminished. Liz admits she is nervous about interviewing, but I assured her that after all she has accomplished, the rest will be a breeze.

Eventually, she will need to continue on for her bachelor's degree, but for now, she can take pride in how far she has come.

Hearing the experiences of some of my students has been rewarding on more than a personal level. There were many who have endured enormous challenges before achieving success. Often in their writing exercises, students reveal how they have had to overcome serious hardships like drug addiction, incarceration and even the pain of physical abuse suffered at the hands of a spouse or parent. My hope is that we can recognize that there is always someone else with greater challenges — like those of Alisha.

Alisha
✳✳✳

Alisha, not her real name, was a student, who asked to remain anonymous because of the personal struggles of her past. She first revealed her troubled past in an essay she had written for class. Later, she opened up to me about the verbal and physical spousal abuse that she endured for eight years before she found the courage to leave with her four children and live with her sister in another state. As Alisha explained:

"It wasn't easy but I owe a lot to my sister for taking us in and always pushing me and encouraging me to stay strong. In time, with the help of government assistance and financial aid, I was able to fulfil my lifelong dream of helping others.

Alisha began by taking courses at the community college and eventually she was able to reach her goals. As she explained,

"This was the beginning of working my way to a better life for my family."

It took Alisha 13 years to achieve her four-year degree, but, it was that degree that has allowed her to secure a job as a social worker where she can help others who face similar challenges. Alisha is a positive role model for her children as well as for others who suffer similar hardships. Her message is simply, "If I was able to do it, anyone can."

Another adult student who has not let his past keep him from achieving his goals is Aimer Garcia.

Aimer
✳✳✳

Aimer Garcia made the decision to reinvent himself after losing his job. This father of two grown children and two grandchildren had decades of experience in the business world but little education. For years he watched others move past him, many of whom had no experience but who possessed college degrees. As Aimer explained to me:

157

"I was doing supervisory work, but because I had no college degree, I could not get the pay or the benefits of a supervisor. I was even asked to train someone to do what I was doing. That person didn't have the experience I had but because he had a college degree, he was able to move ahead of me." I asked Aimer how that made him feel. He continued:

"Back then, I thought there was nothing I could do about it. I had no education other than the high school I attended back in Columbia, South America. Everyone in the United States, who was getting ahead, had college degrees. It wasn't until I lost my job that I realized I had to make changes. There were no decent jobs out there for an uneducated person like me, even with all my experience."

As I listened to Aimer recount his experiences, it was clear that his journey was longer and more difficult than many. Before he could consider higher education, he first had to get through high school. This he accomplished by studying for, and passing, the GED. Aimer knew the next step for him was applying to college, but he had no clue about how or where to begin so he made use of technology. As Aimer explained:

"I didn't know anybody who had done this so I went online and began to research. That brought me to the admissions office where I met a counselor who helped me get started. It was a lot to absorb at first. I had to take a placement test, and I scored very low in math and reading, but I knew that it was now or never. I signed up for a full course load in my first semester and immediately realized that this was going to be tougher than I imagined. Not only did I have to start at the bottom with developmental math, but I also had to learn how to do things the way Americans do them, things like division."

Aimer explained that it had been many years since he had been in school and many of the methods he learned in arithmetic differed from what he was being taught in his math class. Among Aimer's many challenges was his ignorance of technology. Many of his professors posted work on their website forcing him to become a quick learner or, as he put it, "I'd be out of luck."

Life didn't stand still for Aimer as he attended classes. He still maintained a part- time job and needed to spend time with family and time to study, and like most adults trying to multitask, it was his social life that had to be put aside. But he took advantage of what his classes had to offer and the resources available at the college. Within his first semester, he was managing his time better, learning to think and read critically, and benefitting through services like tutoring and financial aid. What began as a Business Management Certificate Program would soon change to a full degree program in Business Management and Accounting. Aimer realized he was capable of "doing this." As he revealed:

"My only regret is I should have tried this sooner because now I know I could have done it. Everything we learn here is for our own benefit. Yes, life gets busy, but, as I tell my daughter and nieces, education is so important. They say they have no time and no money but they spend money on useless things at the mall. They have time and money to go to Manhattan. I try to tell them that they won't work as hard as they do now if they have education."

Aimer is a positive role model for his family, as well as other adults in similar situations. He continues to work hard to reinvent himself. At 48, he exemplifies the essence of my message: "Forget your age, you can do this!"

The adult students I was fortunate to encounter over the years came from all walks of life and backgrounds, yet each possessed a determination that was evident from day one. One of those students who demonstrated his motivation early on was Michael Defrietis.

Michael

***

Michael Defrietis was forced to reconsider his career as a result of a chain of events he described as "a domino effect." I knew I needed to share his story the moment he asked for a favor.

Michael was one of those parents coming to class straight from work. He asked if he could be excused from class on Halloween so he could take his daughters "trick or treating." He assured me he would have his assignment completed in advance. It was evident that he took his schoolwork very seriously, but as he made clear, "Everything I do is for my family."

When I reached out to him requesting that he share his experiences so that more adults could benefit, Michael responded with enthusiasm.

"I'd be happy to do that. I'm still taking courses slowly while I'm working full-time." He added. I asked him how he came to the decision to go to college.

"The economy hurt my family. I was working in construction; work was suffering, and on top of that, I got hurt on the job and needed back surgery. I knew then that I needed to make some major changes to help my family. I needed stability for my family, and I couldn't take years to do something. It was during my recovery that I became motivated to go into nursing." I recalled him saying he needed to do well in English Comp so he could get accepted into the nursing program. Our conversation continued.

"What are you doing now while going to school at night?" I asked.

"Well, for my day job, I'm a plumber. I've been working non-stop since Hurricane Sandy helping people get back to some kind of normalcy. It's been very stressful." I knew exactly what his days were like given the tragedies brought on by Sandy.

"Could you provide details of what it's like to be a full-time student, a husband, a father and a full-time worker?" I asked.

"Thankfully, I have a very supportive wife," he started, "at home, I make every effort to stop whatever I'm doing to respond whenever one of my daughters needs my attention. They are four and eleven and while they try to understand and be supportive, they're still just kids." As Michael continued, I related to his sentiments and reminded him that he was a good example for his daughters.

"On the weekends, I have to lock myself in to get the school work done. Often, my wife has to do things with the kids without me. She gets it, and no one complains, but it's hard." Michael added that he strongly emphasizes the importance of higher education to his children in order for their life to be easier. Then he turned his attention to work.

"Sometimes at work, when I get a lunch break, there's a bunch of us who bring lunch to eat together. Instead, I have to go off on my own to get in some reading for school. I have to squeeze it in whenever I can if I want to get through this." Michael was so aptly describing what so many adult students go through in order to be successful. I asked if he could share some advice for other adults contemplating changes in their lives.

He repeated: "I can't emphasize the importance of higher education enough. I have no regrets with any decisions I've made. It is harder as we get older, but with support and motivation you can do it."

It certainly is harder as we get older, but just as Michael and others have expressed, "support and motivation" can help. Shortly after my talk with Michael, another of my students, Annmarie Allman, would echo those words in our interview as well.

Annmarie

***

On the first evening of class, a few semesters ago, Annmarie Allman announced to me that she was only sitting in for that night as she planned to transfer to another professor's class. By the end of class, she was asking if she could officially transfer into my section because she felt she needed the challenge that I was requiring in Freshman Comp. Later, Annmarie explained she had not read a book in a long time but she assured me she was ready to handle the work required to do well in my class. Annmarie's dedication was evident from the start. Many evenings I would pass by the writing center on my way to class and see her sitting with a tutor working to perfect her paper.

Fifteen weeks later, Annmarie was one of only a handful of students who achieved an A in the course. In our interview she explained:

"I started school in my home country of Grenada but had to finish high school here in the United States. I was 15 years old when I came here. It was like starting all over again. Then, once I decided to go to college, I had to take remedial courses. Again, it was like starting over, but I stuck with it. Your class was tough, but the challenging readings you required helped me in areas of speaking and writing for different subjects as well. Courses like chemistry, and anatomy and physiology, became less intimidating after I was successful in your class."

"Tell me what your life was like before you decided to attend college." I inquired.

"Well, when I got married and had children, **we** moved to Texas, then New York, so it was hard with all of the back-and-forth. I had a full-time job in retail so I didn't think I needed college. Later, with the kids grown and my husband travelling a lot, I needed to do something with my spare time. I also thought about having a career, not just a job, so college was important now."

"Did you have support for your decision?"

"Absolutely, my husband fully supported me. In fact, he recently told me to take a break from work so I could concentrate on the courses needed to get into the nursing program. My daughter was also a big supporter. In fact, we started college together and she would always encourage me to keep going. Their support and motivation help me get through it."

"Tell me how it felt for you to be starting college as an adult."

"It was hard beginning a new venture at 42. At first, I thought I wouldn't fit in and the kids would make fun of me. I needed to work at studying, and every class I took, I doubted myself, thinking I couldn't do it. But my good grades kept me going. The more challenging my classes were, the more disciplined I became. I only accepted As and Bs from myself. In fact, I am on the honor roll now. And next fall I will be accepted into the nursing program."

"That's wonderful, Annmarie!"

"Thank you. The only class I ever got a B in was Anatomy and Physiology II. I was really annoyed about that," she responded.

"You're too hard on yourself. You should be so proud of your accomplishments."

"I know you're right. I really worked very hard. I never missed one class even with the snow in winter and the heat in summer. I just kept going."

"You are a true role model to other students," I replied. "I'd like to end by asking you two more questions. First, do you have any regrets? And second, what advice would you offer to other adults who might be contemplating a life-changing decision?"

Without hesitation, Annmarie began, "I haven't had any regrets; I'd do it all over again. Even with the cooking and cleaning, the laundry, my job and having two children at home, school helped me stay disciplined.

The best advice I would offer others is that age is just a number, and it's never too late to start. If I started earlier, I may not have been ready, so it's ok to wait until the time is right. Also, you have to want to do it; you can't let anybody else decide for you." Then she thought for a moment and added, "Follow your dreams."

Annmarie continues to work hard and follow her own advice. She still keeps in touch with me as she moves closer to her dream, reminding me each semester that she made it through once more.

Working at a college has afforded me numerous opportunities to touch the lives of other struggling adults, both in and out of the classroom. Likewise, hearing their stories has touched me. Often these connections have led to lasting friendships, as was the case with Jeanne and Theresa.

Jeanne

***

Jeanne was a secretary, and later, head clerk in the admissions office. As she was also taking courses as she worked full time, we would often discuss our experiences as adult college students. Like me, and so many others of our generation, Jeanne was raised with the belief that females should marry and become the caretakers. She explained:

"I always had the desire to go to college but my parents were old-fashioned and believed that females should marry young and keep house, cook and sew, and raise a family." As a result, Jeanne accepted their reasoning, and she and Al got engaged at her senior prom and were married just three weeks after her 18th birthday. By 21, she had her first of three sons. Like so many other married women, her life revolved around working, raising three boys and juggling all of the responsibilities that come with being a wife and homemaker.

"How old were you when you first considered college?" I asked.

"I decided to go to college when I was about 39 years old."

"That was the age I was when I first started." I interjected.

"Really! I didn't realize that." Jeanne added.

"Yes, I was 39 when I started at Suffolk. For me, it was about the time that my children were becoming independent of me. They were all in school, or ready to start, and I had no idea what I would do with my future. What about you?" I asked. "Why was the time right for you at that age?"

"There are a couple of reasons I decided to go at that point," Jeanne explained. "For one, I always wanted to further my education, so, as soon as my children were growing less dependent on me, I started to think about college for myself. My oldest son was just starting college, and at about the same time, I began working at the college library where I was expected to use computers. Back then, the field of information technology and word processing was relatively new, and I didn't think my skills were up to par, so, in order to become more proficient at my job, I decided to enroll in a couple of courses."

"You started with two courses while working full-time?" I asked.

"No, I took one course at a time at night," she explained.

"Did you find it fulfilling immediately?"

Jeanne's voice lit up as she recalled with pride, "I did; I caught on right away, and my grades were good. That made me feel good, and I remember thinking, 'I can do this!' I really enjoyed learning."

"Let's talk about your family." I continued. "How old were your children? How did they react to your new venture?"

With a laugh, she recollected. "Well, Brian was 11, and Bobby was 14; neither of them was fazed by it. My oldest son, Ron, on the other hand, had a different reaction. He was 17 and just starting college; all he could think about was running into his mother on campus. I remember him saying, "Please just don't be in the same classes as me, mom. " Jeanne added that her son would either be embarrassed by having his mom in the class or maybe he feared she would be a better student than him. We laughed as I continued with my inquiry.

"What about your husband? Was he supportive of your decisions?"

Without hesitation, she shared, "Al was supportive from the very beginning. He encouraged me every step of the way. Even those times when I was pulling my hair out, thinking that I couldn't get through it, Al would push me with reassuring words like, 'You can do this! You can't give up now!' His support really helped me get through it."

"Tell me about some of those times when you were pulling your hair out," I asked.

Her voice quieted as she recalled, "It happened now and then. There were term papers and tests that caused me stress. But the worst of it was when I was taking statistics. I knew I needed to take math for the degree but kept putting it off. I'm not a mathematical person, and I kept thinking, "When am I ever going to use this?" Of course, that only made it more difficult. Those were the times when I would go home at the end of a long day and feel like I was losing it.

Each semester I was gone from home once or twice a week from 8:30 in the morning until as late as 10:00 p.m. On those nights, my husband and sons would heat up dinners I had prepared in advance for them. When my workday ended at 5:00, I'd go to my car to study or read until my class started at 6:00. My car was the one place where I could find peace and quiet; it became my space to do homework and study during my lunch hours and breaks.

When I was home, I'd make sure the boys' homework was done, take care of the dishes and the laundry then begin my own homework. While I did most of my studying after work, before class began, on nights before a final exam or term paper, I would burn the midnight oil. This was my regimen all along but while I was taking the statistics class, it was intensified."

170

"How was Al able to help you get through this?" I asked.

"Well, he couldn't help me with the math, but he tried to ease my load. He would say things like, 'Forget the dishes, and go study,' then he'd do the dishes or help with the kids' homework while I struggled through the assignments. Al would also remind me of how close I was getting to the end. Of course, he was right; I knew I had to see this through so I sought help through the math tutoring center at the college. The help I received there was invaluable. The tutor was a math instructor who was able to clarify the most difficult problems for me. I don't think I could have gotten through it without her help and Al's support, and constantly seeing the light at the end of the tunnel kept me going until I passed that course."

"Was it difficult to manage financially?" I asked.

"No, because I looked into my benefits and discovered that the county would pay part of my tuition. They actually paid three quarters as long as I continued to take courses that were related to my work. As a result, I decided that I would be able to complete the certificate program."

"That was smart." I added. "It is so important to find out what's out there to ease the financial weight. But you wound up graduating with your associate's degree; when did you make the crossover?" I asked.

171

Jeanne continued, "Once I achieved the certificate, since I was halfway there, I decided to fulfill my lifelong desire to earn a degree, so I continued on towards an associate's degree. Also, during that time, technology was beginning to change so dramatically, that what I had learned had already become obsolete, so it made sense to continue. That's when I decided to go for the business administration degree. By then, I was working in admissions, and that would be helpful to me in the new job and I could continue to get tuition reimbursement."

"Jeanne, I remember you were very involved in the honor society back then. You always seemed very positive and upbeat. Can you talk about some of the highlights of your decision to pursue your education as an adult?"

"There were many," she began. "I remember being inspired by my first English teacher. Funny thing was, at first, I didn't like her teaching methods and wanted to switch to another class. But people who knew me in the registrar told me I should stick it out with her because she was the best in the department. When the course ended, I had to concur and thanked her for helping me become a better writer."

"The pride I felt from my family helped as well. Little things like being able to discuss academics with my son, Bob, made me feel that what I was doing was meaningful. Little by little, my self-confidence was getting stronger."

"I never saw you as someone lacking in self-confidence, Jeanne. You always seemed to be so secure," I stated.

"Oh yes, you didn't know me before I got involved with school and Phi Theta Kappa. I would prefer to stay in the background. The honor society helped me step up and develop my leadership skills. Remember Jack?" She asked.

"Yes, he was a counselor at the college. He still comes in sometimes in the summer to help out." I recalled.

"Well he was the advisor for Phi Theta Kappa and it was he who encouraged me to join. I would go to him for academic advice and course selection, and he kept telling me I would be a great candidate for PTK so I joined, and before long, I was elected PTK president. It was a wonderful experience that exposed me to a bigger world. There were volunteer opportunities, conventions to attend, and the thrill and honor of being awarded one of the U.S. Outstanding PTK Presidents.

"You should be very proud of yourself, Jeanne. It sounds like you have no regrets."

She responded, "No regrets at all! I learned, as you said, I can do this! I loved learning and continue to enjoy it to this day. Even in retirement, I continue to seek out new and interesting things to learn. I've taken a couple of genealogy research courses and have joined a book discussion club. My goal is to become fluent in conversational Spanish. I also try to learn all I can about the Civil War, something I didn't have time for before." Then she added, "Who knows what's next. You can be sure I'll find more!"

Jeanne ended our conversation by reiterating my own message. "Age really doesn't matter, Chris; more adults should believe that they can do whatever they set their mind to." Then she added, "There's an old army motto: *Be all that you can be!* That has always been my own personal motto and one which I always told my kids."

I couldn't have said it better. Because Jeanne's experiences closely paralleled my own, our connection became natural. With Theresa, there were different similarities.

Theresa

***

When Theresa and I sat together at a conference, it was immediately evident that we had much in common, including the struggle to achieve a goal later in life while also juggling the responsibilities that come with being married with three children. Theresa had just completed her academic journey and was looking for a job. Fortunately, I was in a position to keep her in mind when a position opened up in my department. Within two years, I was able to hire Theresa, first part-time, then as a full time counselor for my program.

174

From day one, I observed as Theresa carefully balanced her work with students and her responsibilities at home. She counseled and advised student after student during her work day then left to pick up her young daughter from school. At home, she would check in on her elderly parents who lived downstairs before preparing dinner for the family. I always believed that Theresa must have been the same driven person as a student, and in time, I would find out that my suspicions were correct.

So that others would benefit from her experiences, Theresa didn't hesitate when I asked to tell her story. It is astounding how much one can learn about a person (that is, a person you think you know so well) when one asks questions that require delving deeply into the past and reliving every pertinent experience.

I began as I always do, "How old were you when you first decided to attend college? Why then? Why not before?" Theresa thought back to her high school days before responding.

"In high school, I was interested in art and sewing. I had thoughts of going to FIT, (Fashion Institute of Technology) but life got in the way, so, instead I turned to cosmetology which was another way for me to express my creative interests. By the time I was 28, I was working as a cosmetologist in a salon for 10 years. I had an eleven year old son and a six year old daughter. With a family to raise, I did what I could to help out financially while staying involved with my children."

Theresa spoke with utmost sincerity, displaying sadness, but no regrets, as she continued. I asked her if she could explain what she meant by "life got in the way."

"Well," she continued, "right before high school graduation, Rob and I were married, and shortly after, we had our son. I was a teenage mom before there were reality shows about it."

"That must have been difficult." I interjected.

"It was, but just as difficult was the feeling that I'd disappointed my parents. I recall walking home from church hearing my mom's friends talk about how disappointed Mary must be." As I listened intently, I thought to myself, *Wow that stayed with her all this time.* Theresa explained how she was able to achieve her diploma while at home awaiting the birth. Shortly after, she enrolled in night school for cosmetology.

"Initially," she explained, "I wanted to teach nursery school knowing that FIT was no longer an option, but Robert told me I wouldn't make any money." I knew that well, given my own experience. "So I chose cosmetology school feeling that I could make good money and satisfy my creative interests as well."

"So how did you go from cosmetology to counseling?" I asked.

She explained that her turning point came when she was tutoring in her son's fifth grade class. His teacher, Mrs. Townsend, impressed by Theresa's natural ability to relate to the students, asked why she never considered teaching professionally. Theresa laughed it off, responding:

"I have a family to raise; maybe in my next life." To her surprise, the teacher countered:

"You don't have a next life; you have to do it now!" This left an impression on her the way Abby's response to the writer left on me. Now 29, and totally committed to her family, she wondered how she could do more; she wondered where she would fit more in her structured life. But the seed was planted, and she couldn't shake it off.

While researching the possibilities, she'd heard about programs through BOCES and this new occupational education program starting at the New York Institute of Technology (NYIT). While it piqued her interest, it seemed out of the question, given her family's financial status. Once again, it was the words of wisdom from an educator that helped Theresa decide her fate.

These words came during an interview with the program director, Professor Alfred Shaw. Shortly into their conversation, the professor detected her apprehension, as she confided:

"I don't know if I can do this. I'm afraid to tell my husband." Shaw responded pragmatically, as he explained:

"Let's look at the bottom line here, Theresa. Yes, it will cost you money to get through the program, but in the end, you come away with a degree that will allow you to make much more money than you will have spent to get there. Talk to your husband. Explain it that way to him. I guarantee, he will understand." Theresa listened intently as he continued, "If you look at your daily outlay, I'm sure you can think of some ways to cut corners, and save here and there. Think about it. I believe you are a perfect candidate for my program." Shaw also suggested that she consider working as a sub in skills classes to prepare her for the work ahead and offset some of the expenses.

Following his advice, she was on her way to a bachelor's degree in occupational education. While it all seemed feasible in conversation, she soon found out that her life would never be the same. Her new schedule had her working Monday through Friday as a sub in a skills class and two nights a week and Saturdays in the hair salon. Somewhere in between, she was able to squeeze in her classes and school work.

The hours required her to be out from 7:00 a.m. – 2:30 p.m. She could get her son off to school but what would she do about her daughter. They couldn't afford child care, but fortunately, Theresa found an affordable morning program at the school. After school, a friend offered to let Jasmine come over and wait with her son until Theresa returned home. Now she could take on her new venture with a clear conscience, or so she hoped. As she explained:

"There were times when I needed to make difficult choices that my children couldn't understand. Until this day, my daughter reminds me that I missed "special person's day" when she was in first grade. It still hurts to remember that, but I had to make a choice to take off for her class trip the week before or that. Jasmine and I are very close now, but I still feel bad about it." As Theresa spoke, I could sense her pain.

Once she achieved her associate's degree, Theresa accepted a position as a job coach working with individuals who had various handicaps. She was required to write psychosocial reports on their development and their implementation of the training she provided. She was expected to assist them with shopping, dressing and career placement. Their living conditions left much to be desired; they were needy with many difficulties to overcome daily. She felt so privileged in her own life and wanted to give back to those who were not as fortunate, leading to her decision to become a counselor.

It was also then that Theresa became pregnant with their third child, Chloe. She was 35 years old with an 18 year old son and a 12 year old daughter, and now she was starting all over again. Still, with all the newfound confidence she had acquired through the last eight years, Theresa was not about to allow this to be anything but a joyous occasion to celebrate.

It would be two years later, at 39, before she was ready to continue her education. By then, Theresa's parents had moved into her basement apartment and could help out with childcare, and Rob's schedule was flexible enough to step in when needed. As Theresa put it:

"It was a difficult balancing act; I was still working part time in the salon on the weekends at first, but gave that up when I became a graduate assistant at NYIT. I continued working part time as a service coordinator for United Cerebral Palsy while also attending classes at night, and I did my school work wherever I could fit it in. This was all in addition to being a parent, a wife and a homemaker." She paused, taking time for more reflection, and then continued:

"Halfway through grad school, things looked like they were going to fall apart. My disabilities client died, and I lost my job at UCP, along with my mentor and teacher. Almost immediately after, Robert was laid off from his job. It was devastating at first, but we agreed that it would be counterproductive to leave school unfinished if I wanted to get a job as a counselor."

Theresa persevered, accepting part time jobs along the way until she could complete her master's degree. By then she was 41 but never forgot the advice she'd been given by her son's fifth grade teacher, Mrs. Townsend, "You don't have a next life; you have to do it now."

Like Theresa's, one's journey is often dictated by the circumstances that come up along the way. Multitasking becomes the norm, as was the case with Meryl.

Meryl

***

When Meryl heard that I was writing this book, she could not wait to share her story with me; she knew it would "fit right in," and she was right. Meryl's unique bartering experiences exemplify my premise that "you can do this!"

When she sought to return to school to complete her education, Meryl had two boys, ages three and five. Her husband, a schoolteacher, would just be returning home as she set out to her night classes. With an hour in between his arrival and the

181

time Meryl had to leave, they relied on a friend to look after the boys. Both women had similar circumstances so they formed a buddy system to babysit for each other, Meryl would step in for morning duty, and Jane would cover the afternoon.

This was back in the late 1970s, before cell phones. (Anyone remember that?) So, to stay connected while traveling, Meryl and her husband used walkie-talkie radios. Meryl's handle was "Songbird" and her husband's was "Backpacker." As they travelled in opposite directions, they would discuss the kids, homework, dinner and anything else of importance. As Meryl described it, "We were like two ships passing in the night."

The arrangement worked well until Meryl's friend moved 40 miles away, and the challenges became greater. Meryl could finish her degree if she could take the rest of her classes in the summer but without her friend close by to care for her sons, it seemed impossible. Her 1970 Ford wagon would never withstand the daily commute, and her husband's 1969 Volvo, with 150,000 miles, was no better. But, since Meryl's friend was also losing a babysitter, Jane suggested they all move in together for the summer — a unique solution that would benefit both families.

They shared all of the responsibilities of the household, and five days each week they lived as one big, happy family of four adults, five children and two dogs. The husbands cooked and took care of the kids in the evenings while the wives studied or attended classes. On the weekend, the visiting family would return home to make sure all was well, then on Sunday evening, they would make the trip back.

This allowed both women to complete their degrees and ultimately get jobs. Her story impressed me as Meryl knew it would, and as I was thanking her she quickly interrupted, adding:

"There's more! Before I got a full-time job, I signed up to be a substitute teacher. I needed to start making money after spending so much to get my degrees."

"Didn't you get any aid?" I interjected.

"I did get some aid but we didn't qualify for much. But I was creative and cut corners wherever possible. I knew that if I could just complete my degrees, it would pay off in the end." Now I was intrigued.

"That's what I want to hear about, continue." I said.

Meryl continued. "Well, we drove old cars and never wasted leftovers. Neither of us had any extravagant habits so we were able to manage on his salary but it was getting more and more difficult." I noticed Meryl's expression as she described that time. "But the babysitting was the biggest obstacle to taking classes and working. Through playgroups I began to meet up with other women in similar situations. Some were subbing and taking turns babysitting. I remember thinking that this could be my answer. Before long, I was part of a group of five women taking turns babysitting while the rest subbed."

I interrupted, "I don't understand; how did that work?"

"Well, each of us would get called up usually the night before. We'd communicate with each other as each of us got the call. The last person to be called would turn down the subbing job for that day and take care of all the kids."

"Really? And that worked well?" I asked.

"It worked well until each of us was able to get a full-time job. We all had the opportunity to make good money knowing our children were well taken care of. At times it felt like I'd never reach the end; so many times I felt like giving up. I felt guilty about leaving my boys, even though they were fine. In the end though, it felt good. My sacrifices allowed me to contribute to the better life our boys shared."

I asked Meryl if she had any advice for others. She replied:

"I'd do it all again if I had to. You couldn't have picked a more apropos title for your book," she added, "Forget your age, you can do this!"

Meryl was right. Her experiences reinforced my message in a whole new way. As she explained, she needed to become creative and take part in methods that would allow her to reach her goals. Meryl, along with other men and women of varying ages, discovered that they could do this and make it work! Jackie is one of those women.

Jackie
***

I met Jackie Maclaren when she was in the midst of her pursuit, on summer break. Along with her friends, Sophie and Melissa, she was on holiday in New York City from school, children and work. We became immediate friends with a lot in common; a working mom with three children struggling to balance school and family. Thanks to Facebook and email, we have been able to maintain our friendship, and keep up with the ups and downs of each other's lives. When I learned my friend had graduated from the University of Bedfordshire with her degree in nursing, I couldn't wait to record her experiences.

Like so many of us, Jackie had no support in education as a youngster. Being the second oldest in a family of seven children, her parents had little time to devote to secondary needs and unfortunately, school work fell into that category. As a result, Jackie, "let it slide," as she explained:

"This remains a big regret. I worked part time from the age of 11, before and after school. All I was interested in was money, as this was short in our home. I left high school to work as a baker for two years." This allowed Jackie to save enough money to leave home and move abroad to Gran Canaria where she lived for six years and where, as Jackie put it, "I worked and had the time of my life!" After her return home to Luton, England, Jackie settled into a job as caretaker to the elderly. It was through that job that Jackie discovered her passion, her love of working with the elderly.

Jackie's voice lit up as she reminisced about her work with the elderly. Her passion for her work was evident to me as it was to her employers, as she explained,

"I worked my way up until my company, NHS, said they would pay for me to do my nurse training. It was a three-year course of study. I chose the diploma as it seemed to be the easier option, given my circumstances."

At that point, Jackie was newly divorced. Now, already in her thirties, a single parent with two children, ages three and five, she was beginning a new venture. I wondered out loud how she was able to care for her children while continuing to work and attend classes. Jackie explained:

"In England, if you are a single parent, you get help with child care and living costs. This helped me through some of our training."

Halfway through the course of study Jackie met her partner and became pregnant with her third child. As is the case with most women, motherhood took precedence; also, like most women, Jackie put her own aspirations on hold. After taking the much needed time to welcome and enjoy her son, Jude, Jackie returned to school to complete her studies in nursing at the University of Bedfordshire. I asked her to explain what it was like for her to get back into the routine of work, school and now three children to care for.

"Like you, I felt like giving up many times. To this day, I still do not know how I did it. I actually had to charm my mentors for shifts to fit in with the kids' schedules." Jackie continued. "I've always wanted to be a nurse, but also like you, my family could not support me when I was younger." As Jackie continued, I was reminded of my own experiences. "I like working under pressure." She added.

Jackie recently gave birth to a fourth child, a little girl named Elliot Jean. She explained that she has no regrets and knows now that the end certainly justified all the sacrifices she made along the way. In her words:

"I love the elderly and helping others when they need it most. Being a nurse was all I ever wanted, and although it was hard, I can now say it was worth it."

Life's challenges affect adults in all walks of life, regardless of our gender, our age, or where we live. My friend, Jackie, from across the pond, is no different from the rest of us.

She, too, took the winding road over the straight path to success. She too faced roadblocks along that journey, not the least of which was being a single parent.

So many of the women I spoke to had to work within the limitations of single parenthood; Joan was one of those women.

Joan

***

Joan Tiernan worked with me during my tenure in the college admissions office. Watching her make her way through college as an adult learner was a constant reminder of my own experiences not long before. But, it wasn't until this interview that I realized just how many similarities we shared.

I began the interview with the usual questions leading to the why and how one began their new endeavor when they did. Joan quickly responded:

"My father said, "You're not going. Girls don't go to college!" Even though my mother wanted me to go, I was one of six siblings and so I was expected to get a job and contribute to the family. I always resented that my two brothers were allowed to attend college right out of high school but my sisters and I had to find our own way, years later, to go to college. We were expected to go straight to work after graduation from high school."

Joan's words echoed in me. "Girls don't go to college!" It was the mantra of the 50s and 60s for many of us who grew up in large, middle class families. It wasn't important for girls to have a career. Becoming a housewife and mother was the expected path for us.

Joan continued, "Once I was married, [my husband] Kevin would push me to get my degree. He would bring home the college catalog, wrap it and give it to me as a gift. By then I had lost the motivation and had become more and more intimidated at the thought."

Having worked with Joan for many years, I knew that life threw her a bunch of curve balls. She was 42 when her husband passed away leaving her with two young children, ages 11 and 7, and health issues of her own. She knew, however, that having Social Security would help provide for the boys until they turned 18, thus allowing her to be a stay at home mom for a few years. Having to be both mother and father to the boys left little time or money for Joan to think about anything else.

As Joan explained, "Once my oldest son graduated from high school, in 1999, I decided to look for a full-time job. I took the Civil Service Test and by November, I began working as a clerk typist in the admissions' office at Suffolk County

Community College. Slowly, I began thinking about taking some classes."

It wasn't until Joan turned 50 that she decided that she could do this! As she put it: "This was my birthday present to me! All that time working in an educational setting, talking to students about the importance of education, talking to my two sons about the importance of college, was beginning to open my eyes. I watched you manage school, children and full-time work; counselors and faculty members were always telling me I could do it. I was beginning to see that all of you had more confidence in me than I had in myself."

"So how did you begin?" I asked.

"Well one of the professors recommended an Intro to Human Communications course and that's where I began in the fall of 2002." Before I could ask the next question, Joan was recalling her fear:

"I was petrified entering that classroom the first night. I walked straight to the back of the room and sat down because I didn't want to be stared at. It wasn't long before I realized I had to move. Students were playing on their phones, texting and talking to each other; that was their space, and it wasn't going to work for me. Luckily, the professor put us in assigned seats, and I wound up in front."

"So, when did your fear begin to subside?" I asked.

"Actually, it was that first night when the professor gave us our homework assignment. We had to come prepared to give a two-minute speech about our life for the next class. I remember thinking that two minutes would never be enough for all that I had to say. I was probably the oldest person in the class and had experienced a lot more of life than the others. I was so nervous about speaking in front of the class but I kept reminding myself that all I had to do was speak from experience. I went on so long that the professor cut me off and thanked me for a good job. I think it was his way of nicely saying, "That's enough!""

We both laughed, and I continued: "So, did it get easier from there?"

"No, not really," Joan responded. "I was so insecure yet determined to succeed, I worked double time. I just kept thinking that I can't waste this money; I've got to get through this."

I interjected, "I know how hard you worked, Joan, I watched you go through it each day. Take me through it again." She continued:

"I remember writing constantly. I would take notes in shorthand then decipher them when I got home. If there was a test coming up, I began studying two weeks in advance. I studied during lunch hour, sometimes in my car and sometimes in the conference room. My solace was wherever I could find a quiet space and concentrate. My sons thought I was crazy but it worked for me."

"And it did work for you," I added.

"Yes, it did. In fact, other students in the class would ask to see my notes when the grades came out and they did poorly." Joan recollected with pride.

I knew there was a lot more to her life beyond her job and school so I asked her to think about all of the different roles she played.

"Ok, let's see," she began, "when I started taking classes, Brian was in college and Matthew was in high school. Both boys were living home so I was cooking dinner each night. I was also in charge of the Communion program at my church so I had to attend meetings two nights a week. Weekends were catch-up time. I had to tend to the cleaning and laundry and shopping and whatever else needed to be done as the sole head of the household."

"So you had no support?' I asked.

"Not really, but, I do remember coming home every Monday and Wednesday night to a phone call from my mother." Joan smiled as she recalled her mother's words. "She would say, 'what did we learn tonight, Joan?' That meant so much to me. I knew my mom was so happy I started college. I felt the pride and the confidence she had in me. Sometimes she would add, 'OK, what are we going to take next semester?' I only wish she was alive to see me graduate. But her support really helped me get through the tough times and keep going."

"What were some of those tough times?"

"In the fall of 2005, I felt confident enough to take two classes, but was soon feeling overwhelmed. I chose Group Dynamics and Western Civilization I, both requiring a lot of writing. That was a mistake! To begin with, I hated history. In high school I never applied myself so I did poorly. Now I was taking this history course only because it was required in the degree program. To make matters worse, the adjunct instructor was not a good teacher. He was uncaring and demeaning to students. He would think nothing of embarrassing us in front of the class. When it was time to go to class, I would have a knot in my stomach walking into the classroom. I managed to pass the class with a lot of work on my own. These were the nights that I couldn't wait to get that phone call from my mom to talk about my experiences that night."

Joan continued to recollect with a familiar story. "Then there was that Intro to Literature class. Do you remember when I came to you frantic at the thought of having to write a textual analysis paper?"

I thought for a moment then responded positively as Joan continued to remind me.

"My professor was a very good teacher of literature. I had no idea what a 'textual analysis' was! The problem was my first English teacher was too easy and didn't teach us the different types of essays. Fortunately, I knew you were also teaching writing so I asked you for help. Once you explained and gave me your notes on textual analysis to study, I felt much better. I got an A on that paper and, with some tutoring; I also got an A for the course.

"Yes," I added, "I remember telling you that you that your professor and I both received our training from Stony Brook so you would be fine if you followed my notes."   Joan and I reminisced a bit more, and I asked her about the financial aspects of getting through college.

"So was it difficult for you to afford the tuition or did you have help?"

She explained how the first couple of semesters were reimbursed 75% through her union. "As long as I could demonstrate that the courses were related to my job, I received reimbursement. Since my responsibilities included interaction with students as they entered the college, the communications and psychology courses were helpful. Also, as an administrative assistant, my writing courses could easily be substantiated."

"What about the courses that were not related to your job?" I asked.

"Courses like history, math, and science were not covered. That's when I began looking into other options for aid. Some of my co-workers encouraged me to apply for scholarships that were offered through the college. I applied for as many as I was qualified for and received quite a bit of money as a result. I also filed for financial aid and received some aid for part-time students and some grants."

"That's very impressive!" I responded. "We tell students all the time to apply for everything even if they don't think they will qualify. So often, scholarship money remains uncollected because students don't want to take the time to fill out an application or write a short essay. I'm sure that helped a lot."

"It certainly did!" Joan exclaimed. "I would still be taking courses if I had to pay for everything myself. Instead, I was able to complete the degree — even though it took 10 years — and graduate last year."

I continued, "One last question, Joan. Do you have any regrets?"

She quickly responded, "Actually, yes, I wish I had started sooner! But I'm happy I did it!" Her response was a familiar one but I was glad she ended on a positive note. Listening to Joan's experiences reminded me that there was still another success story that started in the admissions department, Elaine Freilich.

Elaine

***

When I reached out to her, Elaine was happy to recount her journey for me. Before the questions began, I learned that she was almost through her second associate's degree.

"Really? When did that happen?" I asked. I could sense the pride in her voice as she explained her life plan.

"Oh, I finished my first degree, liberal arts, a while ago then decided I'd like to have something different to fall back on when I retire next year so I applied for the paralegal program."

"What a great plan. I had no idea you were studying law. Now, take me back to the beginning. How old were you when you first started, and why then?" Elaine had to think for a moment.

"I was 42 and my main reason for doing this was for my kids. I wanted to show them that if I could do it, they could do it too."

"I'm not surprised." I added. "If there's one thing I remember about you, it's your relationship with your children." I knew Elaine was a single parent of three, working full time, but for a moment I had forgotten how large her extended family was until I asked the next question. "Why didn't you attend college after high school?"

"Are you kidding? There were fourteen of us! We had no money, and nobody told us about financial aid back then. I was number eleven out of fourteen. As soon as I graduated, I had to get a job and help out. College wasn't even a consideration."

"Of course," I continued, "that had to be a challenge in itself for all of you. How did you feel starting this new endeavor at 42?"

"I was scared. I remember the night of my first class. Once I heard we had to write three long book reports, I wanted out. In the beginning, I always second guessed myself. It wasn't until I started taking some classes with Joan that I felt better because now I wasn't the oldest student in the class."

"Tell me about your study habits. How did you find the time to do the work?"

"With a lot of determination," Elaine recalled. "Once I'd begun, I was determined to get this done. I would take my textbooks to bed with me. Instead of reading a novel, I'd read my school work. To this day, tests are the worst for me. Every time I took a test, I wanted to drop the course or drop out altogether, but I knew I couldn't give up and that was that. Then, before I knew it, the course was over and I'd register for another class."

"How difficult was it for you to manage your job, your classes and your children?"

"It was very difficult at times. Every day after school, the kids had to call me to let me know they were home. They always did their homework after school. I would get home shortly after five, and we'd have dinner together. I avoided Thursday night classes so I could continue to be involved in Boy Scouts. Some afternoons, I'd get that call from the kids telling me their dad wasn't coming to pick them up. Then the stress would begin. I'd be at work trying to get someone to go over to be with the kids. Thankfully, I could rely on my sister, RaeAnn, to be there for me and my kids."

"Did you have a lot of support from your family?"

"Not from my ex," she explained, "but my sisters would encourage me and some of my nieces would come by to talk about their classes and ask about mine. We even took a couple of classes together. But RaeAnn was a godsend to me. The kids could always stay with her when I was in a bind. When she passed away, my brother-in-law made sure to keep the contact going with the kids and told me they were always welcomed there."

"What about your own children, how did they react?" I asked.

"They were great. They saw mom going to college, so they were encouraged to go as well. I would tell them about my experiences as a student and how important it was to talk in class, to get involved in discussion. When they'd ask how I did in class, I was always honest even when I bombed a test. That's when I would take the opportunity to explain that doing homework and papers and speaking and answering questions and having good attendance were all just as important to getting a good grade."

"Good advice, Elaine," I noted, then asked, "What about the cost? As a single parent, was it difficult to afford the tuition?"

"I was fortunate to receive financial aid. I also applied for scholarships and got money that way. Any money I received above my costs, I would put towards my children's tuition."

"Is there anything else you'd like to add? Any regrets?" I asked.

"No regrets, I would do it all again, but I think if I'd known all that was available to me, I might have started sooner. But now, I'm almost done and I'll be graduating next May, then retiring after next summer and looking forward to starting new things."

As we ended our conversation, I was reminded that so many of my interviews ended the same way, with pride for having taken on the challenges but with some regret for not having started sooner. Of course I understand the sentiment; I shared the same thinking at times. More importantly, each of us also shared another sentiment – we would do it all again. Even

Muriel, who felt she hadn't gone far enough, had to be proud of what she accomplished.

Muriel

***

When I realized my assistant, Muriel Lanier, had graduated with an associate's degree from our college as an adult student, I asked her to share her experience. She began by saying,

"Children don't do as you say, they do as you do!" Muriel went on to explain that she was going through a divorce at the time. Her daughter was in college, and her son was entering the military, leaving her in an empty house.

She continued, "I needed something to fill the void. I was at the lowest point in my life with no self-confidence. It was time for me now. With divorce, I lost a part of my life; with school, I gained a new part. I loved taking classes!"

Muriel continued to recall her experience. "I would leave work dressed in a suit and go straight to class. Students thought I was the professor. Professors who knew me as the secretary in the college president's office thought I was there to spy on them."

"That's a first, Muriel." I responded as she continued.

"Yes, can you imagine? I guess they didn't think I might want to do something for myself."

200

"What about your children? How did they react to your new-found venture?"

Muriel laughed saying, "They didn't take me serious either at first. They thought I was such a nerd." But her spirit would not be broken. She was just there to do something for herself.

Our conversation continued: "So, tell me about the labor of your day-to-day experiences during that time."

"Well, for me it was a little different. I didn't have a husband or children waiting at home," she reminded me, "but, I did work full time. So, three nights a week, I would leave my office at 5:00 and head straight to class. Often, my classes would take me to 10:00 p.m. Most mornings, I'd return to work bleary eyed, feeling like I never left the campus. But," she added, "I loved every minute of it!"

I asked Muriel how she was able to afford her new endeavor, given her situation. She explained that the financial aspect was the first thing she looked into when making her decision, and fortunately, she learned that her job offered tuition reimbursement. As I've already stated, this is not an uncommon benefit for full-time employees in many agencies. In Muriel's case, there were no restrictions placed on her choice of study but she chose to enhance her current position with the study of business management. As she put it, "It gave me a better understanding of the managerial side of my job."

Talking to me about this time in her life reminded Muriel of just how much her decision to go to college positively changed her life. She began to quote some of her own philosophy as she explained to me:

"I believe there are three Ds in life. They are Divorce, Disability and Death! I made a decision back then that I would not be a victim of any of these if I could help it. I always believed that we must prepare ourselves to stand on our own two feet. Just as I taught my children to always be building their foundation to stand on their own."

I was so impressed with Muriel for all she had done to better herself as well as her children, but then she ended the conversation with a surprisingly negative statement. "Put me down as a failure because I never went on for my B.A. If only I had started sooner."

I responded adamantly that I could not agree that she was a failure, adding:

"An associate's degree is no small accomplishment, not to mention that you did not let your age or your difficult circumstances stand in your way of reaching your goal." Muriel smiled and shrugged tentatively. I knew she was proud of what she had accomplished, and she assured me she had no regrets.

Like so many adults, Muriel was not afforded the opportunity to build her educational foundation earlier in life but she did not let herself become a victim.

Through the help of tuition reimbursement, so many of the adults I've interviewed were able to complete their schooling. Gary Zelhof is another of those adult learners who took advantage of this benefit.

Gary
✳✳✳

My brother, Gary, was always impressed with what I had taken on and once he made the decision to pursue his baccalaureate, also as an adult student, he could empathize with me. Often we would share our frustrations about having to take courses for which we could see no value. I asked Gary to recollect some of the highs and lows of attending college as an adult.

"For one," he began, "as a full-time worker, you don't get to appreciate the full experience of college life. Between working, commuting, attending classes and homework, there was no time for anything beyond the classroom. I worked in uptown Manhattan, took the subway downtown to Pace, where I attended classes, and then took the bus home at night. Most semesters I was in class until at least 10:00 at night. By the time I got home, it was 11:30."

"Those were long days."

"They were, but, in spite of the inconveniences, I maintained a sense of accomplishment. It was my choice to do this, and I knew it wasn't going to be easy."

"What made you decide to go to college as an adult? You already had a good job, didn't you?" I asked.

"In corporate America, no one asks about where you got your degree, only that you have a degree. It helps to have it in your field of work. In my case, it was marketing/management. I did have a good job but it was becoming more and more evident that having a college degree on my resume would help me get ahead, especially with all of the competition I was up against. So I decided it was important to do this for my career. But there was one other factor that motivated me to get through it when things got tough. I kept thinking I needed to set the example for my children. I couldn't expect them to recognize the importance of going to college if I didn't get through it myself."

"That's a sentiment I hear from many adults," I noted before moving to my next subject. "I always encourage people to inquire about tuition assistance through their place of employment. Was that something you were able to take advantage of?"

"Absolutely!" Gary explained. "It would have been much harder and taken much longer if I hadn't taken advantage of the tuition assistance through my company. As long as my studies were in my area of work, they were willing to reimburse me for the courses I took."

I continued. "Can you tell me about some of your biggest challenges going through school?"

"It would have to be finding the time to study. Back then, I was first living in Staten Island with our sister. It was a full house with a lot of activity and noise, making it difficult to find a quiet space to study. I found myself squeezing in the reading on the subway and the bus to-and-from my destinations. When I moved to Connecticut, my commute was longer but I made it work to my advantage by studying on the train. Still, there were papers to write and presentations to give so I had to make time whenever I could on the weekends. Then there was the travelling required for my job. Like you, I carried my school work everywhere."

"Do you have any regrets?" I asked.

Predictably, Gary responded, "Only that I wish I had the opportunity to go to college when I was younger. That's what I will make sure my children have."

Most of us who did not have these opportunities in our younger years share a greater appreciation of the importance of higher education for our own children. Raye was no exception.

Raymonda

***

I've always known my sister-in-law, Raye, to be a very ambitious, creative woman. However, after speaking with her to confirm my facts, I learned a lot more about her fortitude.

Raye's quest for success grew out of a need to finally do something for herself. She could never be classified as the typical stay-at-home mom. As she put it, "I didn't coffee-klatch; I didn't car pool, since the kids walked to school. I took jobs that allowed me to be productive and earn a few dollars but still be around for my family."

She continued, "Artie was off to the city each day looking handsome and spiffy in his pressed suit. His job also required frequent, out of state travel; it may not have been exciting, but he was getting away from the ennui of the day-to-day."

By age 35, Raye was ready to step outside of the homemaker box, at least part-time, taking one art course for one evening each week. What began as a creative outlet for her evolved into an associate's degree in graphic design seven years

206

later. By then, she was 42, but her age was irrelevant. As Raye put it, "Class by class, year by year, the credits accumulated, and I matriculated. Eventually, those credits earned me my first degree."

I was not surprised to learn that Raye's first degree was in graphic design as I always knew her to be very creative and artistically talented but I wondered:

"Knowing how creative you are, I have to ask, why did you switch to library science, Raye?"

"Well, for a while, I worked in a graphics design company, but when that ended, I took a job as a library clerk in the Northport Library. It was there I learned about Empire State's independent study program. That would allow me to continue my studies while working and caring for my family. Within four years, I earned my bachelor's degree.

I was also volunteering one day a week at the Harborfields Library where the director suggested I apply for a trainee position that had just opened. However, it would require enrollment in a library course of study. I didn't hesitate to accept the challenge, but that's when my journey really got tough."

"More than you'd already experienced?" I asked.

"Yes, much more. When I looked into schools with library science, my only choice was Queens College. The hardest part was the drive home at the end of my long days. Most of my classes were back-to-back, beginning at 4:00 in the afternoon and ending around 9:30 at night. I'd been up since 5:30 in the morning with the four children, so naturally there were breakfasts to make, lunches to pack, dinner to prepare, homework to oversee — all the typical tasks that come with family."

"You must have been exhausted," I interjected.

"I was. Some nights it was so bad that I feared getting into an accident and not making it home."

"Were there times when you didn't think you could get through it?"

She hesitated before responding, "It didn't happen often because I was happy with what I was doing. When the thought crossed my mind, I would quickly dismiss it thinking about the money I'd spent on the courses. I was never one to waste anything so to waste money, in this case, was unthinkable. I also had full support from my husband. When he saw I was having doubts, he would say, "Just finish this class." He knew once I'd finish each class, I'd regain my confidence and sign up for another.

But it was in my last semester of college, when I was required to write a thesis, that my endurance was really tested. We had through the summer to complete it, but I had only until September to finish the degree for the library position. I was done in June but my mentor had already left for the summer and wasn't expected back until late August. All I could think of was what if it required more revision, and I couldn't complete it before the September deadline. I was frantic. The stress was so high; I thought I would have a breakdown. I had no choice but to go to the dean of the program to explain my situation and, thankfully, she interceded and got my mentor to come in sooner to review my thesis."

Raye took control of her own fate and made sure she could achieve her desired outcome. I asked her to think about what her experiences meant to her and whether she thought it was worth it. Without hesitation, she replied:

"Without a doubt, it was all worth it. I was able to get a better job and help our children go to college. I can't believe how old the kids got while I was attending school. In fact, we were all college students together for many of the years. When I started in 1977, my children's ages were 3, 8, 10 and 11. When I completed my MLS in 1992, they ranged from 16 to 24. I would say to anyone who might be contemplating a new start, go for it. Start out with something you enjoy, like I did, and see where it can take you."

Raye's excellent advice, stemming from yet another success story, should be considered, especially if you are like many adults who are unsure of a direction to take. Others have a clear direction but need alternate methods to help them reach their goal, as was the case with Raye's husband.

Arthur

***

Arthur Crowe's experience was an extraordinary one. Although unconventional, it epitomizes the non-traditional methods of learning that can be employed for the busy adult with no time to sit in a classroom. He earned his bachelor's degree on the train. That's right! While commuting from Huntington, Long Island to New York City and back, he took classes four days a week through Adelphi University's "College on Wheels Program," also referred to as "Classroom on Wheels" and "Adelphi on Wheels." This innovative program had its tenure from 1971 through 1986, allowing students to earn a baccalaureate degree in various areas of business as well as an MBA. As this was the first I had heard of this program, I asked Arthur to elaborate on his first-hand experience with this unique concept.

"I joined the program in the late 70s and continued to take courses until it ended in 1986. I'd get on the train at 6:50 a.m. in Greenlawn, and the course began in Huntington at 7:00 a.m. ending in Hunter's Point about an hour later."

Still intrigued but uncertain, I asked, "Were these accredited courses?"

"Absolutely! They were no different than the courses taught in the campus classrooms. They were taught by professors who worked at Adelphi and other universities, including NYU. In fact, some of my courses were blended. In other words, the same course would be taught to students going for their MBA and those going for the BA."

"What was a typical semester schedule for you?"

"The courses were each three credits, and they would run Monday/Wednesday and Tuesday/Thursday for an hour in the morning and an hour on the return trip in the afternoon. I was able to accumulate 12 credits in a trimester that way."

"Was it more expensive than attending onsite?" I asked.

"Actually, it wasn't, because we were able to get the student fees waived since we weren't using any of the campus facilities. This was something the commuters fought for and won. As a result, we paid $82 per credit and the cost of books."

I interrupted, "Where did you purchase your books?"

"We got our books on the train. We had to go to Adelphi to register for the course but the books were distributed on the first day of class on the train."

"It sounds like they went to great lengths to make this work for the commuters."

"They really did. We had blackboards and microphones and audio-visual systems, in some cases. The professors either worked in the various fields of business or they were full-time teachers of marketing, accounting and other business courses. We gained a lot of practical knowledge from those who were working in the field and did a lot of networking."

"Why did they stop offering the courses this way?"

"I think the numbers of interested participants just started dropping, so Adelphi later opened a satellite campus on Route 110 in an attempt to make it convenient for commuters to finish."

"That's too bad; it sounds like it was a wonderful alternative for adults who simply had no time to attend college in the traditional manner."

"It really was. In fact, I think it was the first program of its kind in the country, and it worked. After all, we had to commute to our jobs anyway. The hours we spent on the train were now being put to good use. Reading textbooks just replaced reading the newspapers. There were plenty of other railroad cars available for those who didn't want to participate in the learning, but for me, it was the right choice. I was able to earn a degree that otherwise would have taken me years to attain. "

My conversation with Arthur prompted me to do more research on this interesting concept. However, there doesn't seem to be anything like this presently in operation. Just as he thought,

Adelphi University was the first in the nation to pioneer this kind of program. They started with the north shore lines on Long Island and later expanded to the south shore and Metro North which ran from Connecticut to Grand Central in New York City.

Later, in the 1990s, a small college in Boston, Massachusetts started a similar program through their MBTA. That was the most current information I was able to find on this clever concept, most likely usurped by the popularity of online courses, or as my husband, Dave, cleverly put it, "Before online courses became fashionable, people took courses on the train line."

Even with their similarities and differences, each of my interviewees clearly demonstrated how they found creative ways to achieve their desired goals. Still, not everyone could appreciate the benefit of a solid support system, as Nancy and Rene's experiences demonstrate.

Nancy

✳✳✳

Nancy Gerli has been my good friend and colleague for years. As chair of a reading department she, too, deals with the complexity and the anxiety of juggling goals with the frenzy of everyday life.

Nancy thought she had gone as far as she needed in education until discovering that, in order to become a full professor, she would have to complete at least 36 more graduate credits. By then, she was 37, and the thought of starting over again was overwhelming. Of course, sometimes you just do what you have to do, but that doesn't make it any easier.

Like many of us, Nancy had to take her classes in the evening. During the day, she was teaching at the college, meeting with students, grading papers and fitting in the homework assignments from her own classes. Her home life was not unusual. It included a family, children, laundry, cooking and so on. What Nancy quickly realized was that nothing changes when new requirements get added to life.

I asked Nancy, "Since this was a requirement, didn't you receive some release time from your job to take courses?"

Smiling, she explained: "At work, they just care that you get it done; never mind how you manage to get it done. At home, it was my problem to figure out how to fit everything in."

"Didn't you have support at home?" I asked.

"No, I had no support at home. I was constantly being discouraged and told, 'Why do you have to bother doing this? Your job is fine.' Or 'You're not going to make much more money anyway.' At times, I felt I should just forget about it, but deep down, I knew this was something I wanted to do for me. It was a requirement that needed to be fulfilled if I was to move ahead, and I was determined to succeed; I had no choice."

Nancy soon discovered that the road to success was crowded with other adults with similar lives and challenges and in similar need for support. There were single parents with children, adult men and women with full-time jobs, married women and men who were homemakers or caregivers. Most of the adults she encountered ranged in age from 35 to as old as 65. In a short time, she and the other motivated adult students realized they could use their talents to their advantage. What resulted was a study group that doubled as a support group for the participants, as Nancy explained:

"We would get together on campus, before and after class, and when possible, we would expand this unity outside of the college grounds into our homes, libraries, coffee shops, anywhere that was convenient for the group. There were four women and two men in our peer group. Two of the women were homemakers with children, and one was a physical therapist; one of the men was a high school teacher, and the other worked on Wall Street. Each, like me, was up and out early; some as early as 5:00 a.m. and all came straight to class from their jobs."

Often, one or more of us would find it difficult to concentrate, distracted by the stresses of the day, so we'd take time out to listen and talk before getting back to business. There were those times when one of us would lose confidence and want to give up but the group would quickly dispel the fears and doubts, reinstating the necessary self-assurance to continue and not give up."

"Tell me about those times when you felt like giving up." I asked.

"Well, most of the time, I knew I had no choice and I'd fight the urge, but it was hard going home to a full house with no one understanding or caring about what I had to do. Often, I would go home, after a long day of work and class, and find the family waiting for me to cook dinner. No one was willing to pitch in and help me. I was expected to take care of all of them and the house, the cooking, the shopping, and fit in my classes and homework. Balancing everything was a challenge.

I recall this one time when I stopped to pick up groceries, and while I was unpacking the bags, I was getting yelled at for forgetting to buy something. The stress was so bad that I couldn't concentrate on what I had to prepare for class. The next night, I apologized to the group for not fully preparing my part, and they immediately rallied around and helped me complete the task for class.

The people in our group were all very understanding; some had supportive families while others did not and could relate to what I was dealing with at home. They helped me realize that my goals were important."

"It sounds like the members of your group became your only source of support," I observed.

"Oh yes!" Nancy responded. "They helped me overcome the negativity that surrounded me at home and replace it with a positive belief that what I was doing was important. After a while, I came to realize that my aspirations were important, and I didn't have to accept the negative reactions. Of course, that didn't sit well with the family."

"How did they react?" I inquired.

"Well, for instance, one semester I took classes on Saturday mornings and carpooled with two of my friends. When they came to pick me up, I had to make them wait for me outside so as to avoid an argument. But still, I gained strength from the others in the group and in return, I offered support when they needed it. We got each other through it."

Before concluding, Nancy emphasized, "The reason we all were successful, was that every one of us believed that we could do it! Our age didn't matter; our place in life didn't matter. What mattered was our determination and our belief in ourselves and in each other."

Nancy's experiences can help adults understand that the lack of support at home does not have to get in the way of achieving success. You need to ignore the naysayers and instead, like Nancy, you can be creative and find ways of building your own support system.

Rene

***

Rene's story needed to be shared for so many women and men who believe there is no way to overcome the barriers of indifference and lack of support they face at home. A support system is important, but as she demonstrates, the lack of it does not, and should, not deter one from reaching a desired goal.

Rene was 19 when she married and moved from Ohio to New York with her husband's family. As the middle child in a family of 12, she was taught early the importance of education by her own college-educated parents. However, her new life proved different in many ways. Now she had to acclimate into a family who placed little importance on formal education. As Rene put it, "In many ways, my experiences were those that most first generation students have to face even though I wasn't a first generation student."

Rene began her academic journey before her marriage and the birth of her son. Throughout the years that she attended college, for a bachelor of arts and a master's, Rene had two more children. With each child, it got more difficult but she was determined to continue her schooling even if it took her 20 years to complete.

I asked Rene about childcare when her children were young. "Well," she began, "we lived with my in-laws, and my mother-in-law was happy to take care of my son on days I had class. I tried to keep it to four days a week, a few hours each day."

"That must have been convenient for you."

"It was convenient most of the time, but it was hard to regain control when I was home. I found myself trying to please everyone while also trying to keep up with the housekeeping, studying and class projects. Then, when we were able to get a place of our own, my mother-in-law was very upset that we were taking my son away from her. She kept saying that she had raised him, and how could we do this to her. It really hurt to hear that."

"Do you think the difference in culture contributed to that?"

"I do think it had a lot to do with it. My in-laws didn't go to college. My father-in-law never went to school, and my mother-in-law only went to school through eighth grade. Being from the Middle East, they didn't understand the pressure in the

United States to attend college; they also didn't appreciate what I was dealing with as a student, a wife and parent."

"I'm beginning to see your affinity with first generation students, Rene. What about your husband, was he supportive of you through those years?"

"At times I felt he was but then there were times when it seemed he was supportive only when it was convenient. I remember this one time when my mother-in-law couldn't babysit, and my husband was going to fill in. I had a paper to present that day in class. I spent the morning editing and printing my work while waiting for my husband to return from Manhattan where he was helping my father-in-law with something. He knew I was counting on him and how important this was to me. As the morning progressed, my stress was building. I couldn't take a shower because I didn't want to leave my son alone. I knew the whole class was dependent on me to lead the presentation. I thought about calling the professor to give him a heads-up but then I kept thinking my husband would arrive any minute. Unfortunately, that was wishful thinking; he showed up just 20 minutes before my class was to start with no explanation and no second thought about my need. Without a word between us, I bolted out of the house, no shower, paper in hand and angry that he had done this to me."

"Did you make it in time to give the presentation?"

"I did, but I felt so self-conscious while giving my presentation because I hadn't taken a shower. I thought my husband understood how important my academics were to me, but I soon realized that he really didn't care."

"What happened to make you feel that way?" I asked.

"There wasn't any one thing," Rene explained. "I just knew that if I was going to get through this, I had to find ways to make it work without relying on my husband."

"Tell me what it was like when you moved from your mother-in-law's house. Who took care of the children?"

"When we moved into an apartment complex in Stony Brook, I had three young children. Most of my classes were in the evening when my husband was working so I would travel from Stony Brook back to Kings Park to leave the children with my mother-in-law. From there, I would drive to Stony Brook to attend classes then back to Kings Park to pick up the children around 10:00 at night then back home. Once I got home, I would carry my daughter into the house while my other daughter and son were locked in the car. With my younger daughter in bed, I'd go back out and pick up my other daughter and carry her into the house. Then I did the same with my son.

I did this two to three nights a week for a number of years while I took classes at night for my master's degree. To write my thesis, I took a different approach. I found a babysitter in the apartment complex, and found a way to pay her for several hours in the daytime while I translated and wrote commentary, got feedback from my peer readers, and met with my advisor. I never spoke to my husband or his family about doing this. I knew they would never have understood. It took me five years to earn my M.A."

"In spite of the lack of support, you succeeded in reaching your goal," I noted.

Rene quickly interjected, "Yes, but ironically, I found I was most propelled forward when I received the least amount of support from my husband and his family. That was how I was able to get through grad school and eventually earn my Ph.D."

Before I asked, Rene was reliving her experience for me.

"After I completed my master's, I taught in high school but soon realized it wasn't for me, so I started teaching as an adjunct at Suffolk Community College. I had already been teaching courses at Stony Brook University as a grad student. I knew I could never get a full-time job without a Ph.D. but I didn't see how I could accomplish that with three children and no support from my husband. As far as he was concerned, I was done with school. Unfortunately, that became my thinking too. It was my mentor/advisor at Stony Brook, who I still visited regularly, who helped me see the possibilities. She recognized my potential and understood my challenges. She just looked at me one day and said, 'Why don't you go for the Ph.D.?'

By then, things weren't going well between my husband and me, and I knew I needed to prepare myself to be self-sufficient. There were times when I wanted to quit, but the need to get through it was stronger than the stress. I knew I had to remain focused if I was to achieve my goal. I applied to the Ph.D. program in comparative literature and got accepted. By the time I began my first semester in the program, I had found a way to live on my own, and we were separated."

"How did you pay for the classes without his help?"

"Well, I was still teaching so I was able to use some of the money I had saved from that. Then, once I was working on my dissertation, my children were all in school, and I started teaching four classes each semester."

Rene's academic journey spanned 20 years. With limited choices and little support, she was able to achieve her Ph.D. Through it all, she found strength she did not know she had. When I asked Rene if she had any regrets, she explained:

"There were times throughout the journey that I questioned myself, but in the end, I realized the importance of what I had accomplished. I know my three children see me as a role model for how to be persistent when striving to reach their goals. I've remarried and now have a supportive husband who appreciates my academic pursuits and the importance of pursuing my passions."

Rene's experience can benefit many adults who have the passion to pursue a dream but lack the support of their loved ones. As I noted earlier, you need to accept the support wherever you can find it because there will always be those who will make you question your choices. Rather than let these people influence your decisions, use their words to fuel your fire, and work harder to reach your goals.

As you know by now, I believe strongly that age is just a number. I've tried to demonstrate a common thread among the people I've quoted here and throughout the book. Each has demonstrated the belief expressed by motivational speaker, Denis Waitley: "There are two primary choices in life: to accept conditions as they exist, or accept the responsibility for changing them."

We cannot do everything at once, but we can do something at once.

Calvin Coolidge

Chapter 23

What will you do now?

So, you've read my story, along with those of others like me. You've read about the pitfalls and advantages of getting started on your dream. Now what are you going to do about it? By now, you should have determined what the "it" is for you. Since most careers require some amount of college, you need to remain focused on this path. I suggest you go online, and search the website of the college you are likely to attend, and start finding your answers.

Most of what you need to know can be found online, at least enough to get you started. For example, you should begin by checking the college calendar to determine the start of the semester. This can also help you plan around your children's school schedules. When does the semester end? What are the dates of the holiday break and winter recess and spring break? Do they coincide with those of the district school your children attend?

You will also want to find out if you need an entrance exam before beginning classes. If testing is required, think about how you can prepare for this. A lot of colleges will offer links to test preparation websites or sample practice tests. If this is not the case, you can practice by taking sample SAT tests. Since that is a national test, and it helps prepare high school students for college, you can't go wrong. You can pick up an SAT prep guide at your local library if you don't want to purchase it new.

Some college prep tests can be found by searching the name through Google, Yahoo or other search engines. For instance, a well-known test used in many community colleges is Accuplacer. They offer sample test questions online to help you prepare for the actual test. Keep in mind, how you perform on these tests will determine the courses you are required to take in your first semester.

College placement testing is required for the express purpose of determining if you are ready for college-level courses. These exams test your aptitude in the areas of reading, English and math. For most adults, these are subjects that have not been practiced since high school. Also for most of us, high school could be twenty or more years ago. That is not to say that you haven't done any reading since high school. Most probably, if you are like me, you read newspapers or magazines or novels often, but have read any challenging, college-level material? For example, readings like Shakespeare or Plato's *Republic* or Dante's *Divine Comedy* are not uncommon to expect in an English class.

When it comes to aptitude in the area of English or writing, for many in today's technological generation, skills are limited to email, texting, Facebook and Twitter. But how are you at writing a research paper or a textual analysis? How is your grammar and sentence structure? I mention these to help you understand why these college placement tests may be necessary and helpful.

Something else to note is that these entrance tests are usually only required for students who are matriculated in a program. You shouldn't feel uncomfortable if you don't know what that means. After all, why would you? Before I started taking classes, there were many terms, like this, that I'd never heard before. Students who are matriculated have been accepted into a degree program in college. Students who are non-matriculated are taking courses but have not been accepted (or have not applied) to a specific degree program. Some prefer to begin by just taking a couple of courses before deciding on a program that piques their interest. In this case, some colleges will not require placement testing. The only way to determine the requirements expected of you is to do the research for the school you wish to attend.

Once you have begun your research, look for the application on the college website, fill it out, and send it in. This can usually be done electronically, through the mail or in person. You will most likely be required to supply an official high school and/or college transcript along with a health record.

Another step that should be taken as soon as you've made your decision is filing for financial aid. Since this is money granted through the federal or state government, the forms can be downloaded online. My best advice to you is this: Do not assume you will not qualify for any aid, just fill out the forms, and find out for sure. Even if you don't qualify for aid, you can qualify for student loans which will be at rates lower than a bank, and you will not be expected to pay back the money until after you have completed all of your schooling and graduated.

If all of this seems overwhelming to you, then at the very least, take a ride to the college, and head for the admissions office. Most will not require an appointment, but be sure to ask to sit down with someone so you can comfortably ask all of your questions. This is your time, so don't be shy or intimidated. If you think you might forget or feel awkward, bring a list with you of the things you are unsure of. Don't make the same mistake I made. Don't allow your fear to guide you; instead, remind yourself why you are there. At that moment, when you are sitting across the desk from an advisor, questioning yourself, wishing you could just crawl under the desk, I want you to think of me. Picture me waiting in lines while trying to entertain three little children or standing at the registrar counter, while trying to corral the three kids, just to request a catalog. Think about what I said to you in my introduction: "I was the person you are." Then I want you to think of me now, with years of schooling behind me, and remember that I am the person you can be.

Insanity: Doing the same thing over and over again and expecting different results.

Albert Einstein

Final Thoughts

It's Okay to Start Slow, But, Just Start!

Some of you may still be thinking that this is all too overwhelming. I can understand that because this book is about awakening the passion in you and bringing it to life. Not everyone desires to reach the end of their proverbial rainbow. Some may just want to feel better about themselves in some small way. Some may not be ready to take that major leap; instead, they may prefer to wade. For some of you, small changes may be enough. My message is the same for you; just get started, and do something for you!

How, where, when, you ask? Go to your computer, pick a search engine like Yahoo, Google etc. and type in "adult classes." Add your city or town, and you will be amazed at how many options are out there for you. They range in size and cost, but there is something for everyone. Courses and classes range from physical fitness classes to art classes, to computer classes, and on and on. Many colleges and libraries offer free classes in just about every subject area.

Maybe you've been contemplating a business venture. Many of these same resources can assist you with getting started. Just remember, when I say you need to forget your age and that you can do this, the "this" is anything you want it to be; it is anything you aspire to, anything you've thought about doing but think you are too old to start. You are not too old! Forget your age! You can do this!

Appendix

We often view the success of others with little thought about how they got there. Failure and success knows no age. By now, you should be convinced that it is how you react to failure that will determine your ability to achieve success. But, in case you still doubt yourself, here are some experiences of familiar people who have reached success in spite of their obstacles and failures.

Most are familiar with Oprah Winfrey, best known for her incredible success and generosity. What many may not realize is that her early life was one of poverty and abuse. In an interview with Julie Chen from CBS, Ms. Winfrey revealed her early beginnings. Born to unwed parents, she spent her early years with a grandmother who instilled in her, the values of hard work and excellence. After her grandmother died, at age six, Oprah lived with her single mother, on welfare, in a two room apartment. During this time, she was sexually abused by a relative. It was when she was taken in by her father, that she was taught the importance of discipline and education. Oprah also revealed this information, on her television show in 1986, in an effort to help others who suffer the pain of sexual abuse.

While still in college, Ms. Winfrey was offered a job as a television news anchor but it wasn't her passion, and as she explained to Ms. Chen, her "energy flowed better after being fired from that job." It was the local talk show in Baltimore that would be the beginning of Oprah's journey to greatness. In spite of all she's been through, Ms. Winfrey continues to demonstrate her own belief that, "Failure is a stepping stone to greatness."

***

In 2013, the news media covered a wonderful human interest story about an endurance swimmer who completed a record breaking swim from Cuba to Florida. Dyana Nyak made her first unsuccessful attempt in 1978 at age 28. In 2011 and 2012, she tried three more times, still unsuccessfully. Then on September 2, 2013, at the age of 64, after swimming for 53 hours, without a shark cage but accompanied by a support team who monitored her along the way, Dyana reached the shores of Florida.

Dyana's accomplishment speaks for itself. After five attempts, 35 years after her first try, she overcame the odds and achieved her lifelong dream. It was inspiring to watch as she reached the shore, and she had this to say: "I have three messages. One is, we should never ever give up. Two is, you are never are too old to chase your dreams. Three is, it looks like a solitary sport but it's a team." Certainly her feat is proof of what can be accomplished with determination and continuous effort.

***

You may be familiar with the actor, Mandy Patinkin, from the series, *Homeland.* Mr. Patinkin also starred in *Criminal Minds*, a series about FBI profilers of horrific serial killers. I bring him up because, as an actor, his experiences embody my message of accepting failure and moving forward to achieve success.

Fans of *Criminal Minds* will remember that his departure was sudden and unexpected. Later, viewers would learn that, because he took his leading role so seriously, the content became personally disturbing to the point where he could no longer cope with it, so he walked away. In an interview with Alex Witchel, for *New York Times Magazine*, Patinkin explained that after that unfortunate occurrence, "[he] never expected to work in television again," adding, "If you ask me, 'You're 60, what's one of the best things you've picked up on?' Two things I would say. One is stop trying to be Superman. Allow yourself to make mistakes and serve the team. . ."

Later, he apologized to the cast and returned to make it right in a final scene. His subsequent success in *Homeland* is proof that failing, or falling now and then, need not be the end, as it sometimes appears. Patinkin put his whole being into a role that, as he said, ". . . was not the right fit;" still, he was able to recognize that he could no longer handle playing a role that was distressing him.

***

A second lesson can be learned here. We should recognize when the decisions we make are not right for us. Whether it is a program in college or a job, it is important to be comfortable with our choice and not stick with it for the wrong reasons. That is not to say we should give up, but instead, we should make the necessary changes toward finding what is right.

Anna Mary Robertson, better known in the art world as Grandma Moses, found her true calling as an American folk artist very late in life. In "9 Women Who Succeeded Later in Life," an article written for the *Huffington Post*, Julie Zeilinger explained how Robertson was in her late 60s when she realized she could no longer handle the toil of farm work so she took up embroidery to fill her time. She enjoyed creating pictures through embroidery until arthritis forced her to give up this relished pastime. It was then, at age 76, that Grandma Moses turned to oil painting.

In her obituary, sited in *The New York Times*, we learn how, in the beginning, painting pictures that portrayed her life in rural New York was just another enjoyable way to fill her time. She displayed her paintings, alongside pickles for sale at county fairs and in the local drugstore. It was there that an art collector, visiting from New York City, saw the paintings and bought all that were on display. On his recommendation, some of Moses' paintings were included in an exhibit titled, "Contemporary Unknown American Artists," at the Museum of Modern Art in New York City.

At each stage of her life, Ms. Robertson sought new pastimes when she realized that she could no longer handle the task at hand. Anna Mary Robertson remains an inspiration to all who wish to try new ventures at any age.

Walt Disney is another famous personality who has become a household name throughout the world. What most people don't know is that he had to endure much failure before achieving fame and fortune. According to an article, in the *Kansas City Star* entitled "Our Famous Employees," Disney delivered copies of the paper as a boy, but when he applied for positions "as a cartoonist, clerk and even truck driver . . . the newspaper turned him down each time."

His drive and determination propelled him to explore his talents in animation and start his own business. However, soon after, the company fell into debt and went bankrupt. Still determined to succeed, Disney continued with his animation and the creation of short cartoons, but this ended in contract disputes causing him, once again, to have to start over.

Many books have been written about Walt Disney, each telling the same story of his drive and determination. Most people would have fallen to the belief that after three strikes, you're out; instead, Disney persevered, turning his defeats into triumphs. The creation of Mickey Mouse was the beginning of his enduring success.

***

Similarly, writer Stephen King had to face rejection after rejection before his first novel, *Carrie,* was published. After 30 rejections of the then short story, King gave up and threw it in the trash. As he explained in an interview with Mark Lawson from the BBC, "I was teaching . . . and the money constraints presented a problem, and so I threw *Carrie* away, and my wife fished it out of the wastebasket and said you ought to go on. She read it after she fished it out and brushed off the cigarette butts . . . she liked it." Fortunately, King took her advice and continued to work on the story, turning it into a novel and submitting it to Doubleday. Shortly after, the publisher sold the paperback rights for $400,000 earning King half that amount.

Had it not been for the support and encouragement of his wife, Stephen King may not have become the prolific writer we know today. In his literary career, he has written more than fifty novels selling in excess of 350 million copies.

In every field there are success stories of those who have had to overcome defeat and rejection before reaching success. When it comes to success in motion pictures, the name Steven Spielberg is at the top of the list. With films like *Jaws, Saving Private Ryan, Schindler's List, Raiders of the Lost Ark, The Color Purple* and many, many more to his credit, Spielberg is one of the most popular filmmakers of all time. Yet, this successful writer, producer and director of more than 150 films, was rejected three times from the University of Southern California's School of Cinematic Arts. Determined to succeed in his chosen field, Spielberg enrolled in California State University Long Beach.

Years later, in 1994, he became a trustee and was awarded an honorary doctorate from the same school that originally rejected him. In 2009, at an unveiling of the new film school at

USC, Spielberg was quoted by *USA Today*, saying, "As you know, I have tried to have some association with this school, but eventually I had to buy my way in."

I have been fortunate to know many adults who took the long and winding road to complete their journey. They, like many I have never known personally, have helped me along my own journey. So, it is fitting to end with the experience of an impressive Yugoslavian immigrant who exemplifies the message of this book.

***

Gac Filipaj made news when he earned his baccalaureate from Columbia University where he worked as a janitor. Chris Wragge, CBS news anchor, interviewed the Dean of the School of General Studies, Peter Awn who proudly stated, "For Columbia, this is one of the great, great stories." Indeed, this is a great story. Gac Filipaj epitomizes the American Dream shared by so many. He has proven to himself and others that with hard work and determination, one can overcome obstacles and achieve success.

Mr. Filipaj was 32 when he came to this country from his native Yugoslavia, not speaking a word of English. It took him seven years to learn English well enough to be accepted into

Columbia's classics program where he studied Greek and Latin during the day and cleaned bathrooms at night.

He spent a total of 19 years attending classes while working full time, then, at the age of 52, his perseverance paid off. Gac Filipaj earned his bachelor of arts in classical studies from Columbia University, with honors. I watched as the story of his success was featured on many news programs and I could not help but be inspired. What resonated with me were his words, spoken just days before he graduated in 2012, "To be honest with you, sometimes I think I do not fit in there because of my age, but then I think, Why not!" Why not, indeed!

Rejection, defeat and insecurity can have a debilitating effect on some people. Sometimes it seems easier to give up. I have certainly considered it many times throughout my journey. After all, it takes a lot of hard work to reach success. Every person I have referenced in this book is proof of that. Yet, every one of them, whether famous or not famous, rich or poor, young or old, is an example of how hard work and determination can beget success. In their own ways, each person cited in these pages is saying, "Forget your age, you can do this!"

To all adults who struggle to reach a goal, at any age, I hope this book serves as a motivation and affirmation that You Can Do This!

Chris Crowe

Acknowledgements

To my family, friends, colleagues and students, who are too many to name, thank you for allowing me to delve into your personal struggles, and share them in this book, so that so many others can be motivated and inspired by your experiences.

To Alexandra Belanich, thank you for the tireless work you put in to helping me edit this book. Even when I was sure I had gotten it right, you helped me make it better.

To Ming Gullo, thank you for your expertise with the interior formatting. You alleviated my frustrations and made a difficult task seem effortless.

To the publishing representatives who motivated me to go forward, even when it didn't fit their criteria, thank you for encouraging me to tell my story.

Made in the USA
San Bernardino, CA
23 December 2015